kids'
baking

hamlyn

kids'
baking

60 DELICIOUS RECIPES
FOR CHILDREN TO MAKE

Sara Lewis

For Mitch, an enthusiastic and creative cake maker and taster.

First published in Great Britain in 2006
by Hamlyn, a division of Octopus Publishing Group Ltd
2-4 Heron Quays, London E14 4JP

Copyright © Octopus Publishing Group Ltd 2006

ISBN-13: 978-0-600-61403-6
ISBN-10: 0-600-61403-4

A CIP catalogue record for this book is available from the British Library.

Printed and bound in China

10 9 8 7 6 5 4 3

Notes

Standard level spoon measures are used in all recipes:
1 tablespoon = one 15 ml spoon
1 teaspoon = one 5 ml spoon

Both metric and imperial measurements are given for the recipes. Use one set of measures only, not a mixture of both.

Ovens should be preheated to the specified temperature. If using a fan-assisted oven, follow the manufacturer's instructions for adjusting the time and temperature.

Medium eggs have been used throughout.

A few recipes include nuts and nut derivatives. Anyone with a known nut allergy must avoid these. Children under the age of 3 with a family history of nut allergy, asthma, eczema or any type of allergy are also advised to avoid eating dishes which contain nuts. Do not give whole nuts or seeds to any child under 5 because of the risk of choking.

Key

The apron symbol indicates recipes that are suitable for young or new cooks.

contents

introduction

baking with kids

What better way to relax with your child than to share the joy of making and baking cakes, cookies or bread. The smell alone is wonderful as it drifts through the house and the compliments your child will reap will make them burst with pride, whether they are a young pre-schooler or a teenager with attitude. There are recipes for all ages and abilities – from easy all-in-one cakes ideal for the very young cook, and quick cakes to make after school, to something a little more ambitious for the older cook, such as some of the special cakes in the 'Cakes to impress' chapter.

Cooking isn't just fun, it's educational, too, without your children even noticing it! Weighing out ingredients helps with basic maths – from simple addition to fractions, not to mention the all-important skills of accuracy and attention to detail. In addition, mixing, spreading and spooning all help with coordination. As your child grows in confidence and experience, parental input can become less and less, thereby increasing your child's independence and self-esteem.

For those children who are very fussy eaters, cooking can also encourage them to be more adventurous, to try foods as they prepare them and to inspire a love of food rather than the dread of stressful mealtime battles.

With more and more supermarkets stocking greater numbers of ready meals, we are in danger of bringing up a generation of children who can't or don't want to cook, preferring to sit in front of the TV or computer instead. Cooking at school is no longer an option for many children so it is up to us as parents or grandparents to encourage our children to want to learn. Luckily for me, I had a mum who let me take over the kitchen with my friend on a Saturday afternoon. We made a terrible mess and had a few disasters but always enjoyed tasting the end results. My own children love to cook – my daughter Alice keeps making muffins to soothe her exam nerves while my young son William is a griddle cake and chocolate spread fan.

Unlike many other activities you may do with your children, you don't need to travel, queue up, pay for classes or buy lots of specialist equipment to enjoy cooking at home. The chances are you will have most of the ingredients in the cupboard and you can eat the end result. So get baking together and have fun!

Sara Lewis

kids in the kitchen

Baking is great fun for everyone but if you're planning to cook by yourself, always check with an adult before you begin. Make sure that you have all the necessary ingredients and all the right equipment, especially the right size cake tin (see page 12), before you start.

getting started

First choose a recipe you would like to bake and make sure that you have the time to prepare and cook it – this is especially important if you are going out later. Collect together all the ingredients and equipment you will need. Turn on the oven so that it can be heating up ready for cooking, then begin measuring and weighing out your ingredients and away you go!

hygiene and safety

Don't forget the following basic hygiene and safety rules when working in the kitchen:
- Always wash your hands before you begin.
- Tie back long hair.
- Wear an apron or old shirt to keep your clothes clean.
- Only use food that is within its 'use-by' date and throw away any food that has been dropped on the floor.
- Make sure you have an adult with you when using sharp knives, electrical equipment or the cooker.
- Enjoy yourself cooking but don't play about in the kitchen or you could hurt yourself, as well as spoiling the recipe.

- If you're not sure what size saucepan to use, then choose a bigger one so that its contents will be less likely to boil over. Turn saucepan handles to the side of the cooker, to avoid them being knocked as you pass by.
- Wipe up any spilt food or liquids on the floor at once to avoid slipping on a greasy patch.
- Always use oven gloves when taking hot dishes out of the oven.
- Avoid damaging the work surface with sharp knives or hot dishes – always chop or cut food on a chopping board and put hot baking tins or saucepans on a heatproof mat, a wooden chopping board, or even the hob as long as nothing is cooking on it.

clearing up!

The tidying up afterwards is not as fun as cooking but it has to be done! Make sure you put away all unused ingredients, wash up and dry all the equipment you have used and wipe all the work surfaces with a clean damp cloth before you leave the kitchen. Then hang up any wet tea towels to dry.

Don't forget to sweep the floor, too, as there are sure to be some floury and sticky bits, and remember to turn off the oven when you have finished with it.

cooking with very little children

Young children need supervision in the kitchen at all times. Stand your child on a sturdy chair so that he or she can reach the work surface or sink. Alternatively, cover the floor with a plastic or PVC tablecloth then get the child to measure and mix while sitting on the cloth.

Some little children hate the feel of PVC aprons. If you don't have a cotton one that's small enough then use an old shirt of an older brother or sister as a cover up. Remember to allow plenty of time for your cooking as children hate to be hurried.

When the cooking's done, it's good practice to involve little ones in the clearing up, too. Even tiny children can have a go at washing up if you give them plenty of time and encouragement and keep the mop handy for sorting out any spills.

kitchen equipment

The required equipment (and ingredients) are listed in order of use throughout the recipes in this book. Most of the equipment needed for baking will be things you already have at home. Microwaves and electric mixers have been given as options to help save time and effort but are not essential.

weighing and measuring

Accurate weighing and measuring is very important. If you don't measure and weigh out your ingredients carefully the recipes won't work!

It doesn't matter whether you work in metric (grams, millilitres and litres) or imperial units (pounds, ounces and pints) but you must stick to just one kind – don't mix and match or the recipe may not work.

scales

Digital add-and-weigh scales are the easiest and clearest to use as the amount is shown as a number with pinpoint accuracy, whereas balance scales need a little more skill.

measuring spoons

If you don't already have a set of plastic or metal measuring spoons then these are a must. Fill the spoon with the ingredient then level the top with the back of a knife. Don't be tempted to use a rounded measure as this may give you almost double the amount of ingredient that the recipe actually needs. Everyday cutlery should not be used for measuring as the designs, depths and shapes of the spoons vary so much.

measuring jugs

Use either a plastic or a heavy-duty glass jug. Fill it to the required level then double-check the quantity by setting the jug on a hard surface so that the contents are level.

mixing

Most homes will have a clear-glass or plastic bowl suitable for mixing ingredients in. If you are short of bowls then use cereal bowls for small amounts or a large casserole dish for mixing.

Always use a wooden spoon to stir ingredients being heated in a saucepan as metal spoons become too hot to hold and will also damage the surface of a nonstick saucepan.

using a microwave

Microwaves are great for saving time, especially when softening butter or melting chocolate. Always use china, plastic or heavy glass bowls in the microwave. Don't use metal containers or dishes with silver or gold decoration as these will make sparks when the microwave is turned on.

using an electric mixer

A hand-held electric whisk is probably the easiest electrical gadget worth having in the kitchen. It saves a lot of time, especially when creaming butter and sugar together, whisking egg whites or whipping cream.

Carefully fix the two metal beaters in place before you switch on the whisk or the beaters may fall out in the middle of mixing. Do turn off the electricity before you take them out to wash.

If you use a food processor instead, then fit it with the plastic blade before use. The powerful motor makes light work of mixing cakes and, unlike with a hand-held mixer, any flour that may fly up during mixing is kept in the bowl beneath the tight-fitting lid. If adding fruit to the mixture then mix it very briefly for just a matter of seconds or the fruit will be very finely chopped and lose all definition in the cake.

OVEN KNOW-HOW

- Although all ovens are supposed to run at a certain temperature, many run slightly hotter or colder so check with a parent before you begin cooking. Fan-assisted ovens always run hotter so reduce the temperature or cooking time slightly, according to the manufacturer's instructions.

- Cook cakes on the centre oven shelf.

- Check on the cake's progress towards the end of cooking time and if it looks done, even though there is still time to run then test it (see page 18). If it still needs longer but you feel it might overbrown, then cover the top loosely with a piece of foil and put back in the oven.

- When making a large cake don't be tempted to open the oven door until at least halfway through the cooking time, or the cake will sink because of the rush of cold air that hits it.

cake tins

You will see from the recipes that you can use all sorts of tins in which to make cakes – from roasting tins and flan tins to the more traditional cake tins. For baking cookies and some breads, you need only one or two good-quality baking sheets.

choosing your tin

The number of different cake tins listed in the box opposite seems high, but remember that there are 60 recipes in this book, which is a lot of different cakes, cookies and loaves!

If you don't have the right size of tin improvise with what you do have, but check on the cake's progress in the oven. The larger the tin, the thinner the cake will be and the less cooking time it will require.

If you want to use a square tin instead of a round one then go down a size. For example, if the recipe calls for a 20 cm (8 inch) round tin, then the cake mixture will also fit into an 18 cm (7 inch) square tin.

lining cake tins

Unless you use cake tins with a nonstick surface it is usually best to line at least the base of the tin with a piece of lining paper.

You can use nonstick baking paper or greaseproof paper to line cake tins. The difference is that nonstick baking paper, or parchment, has been specially treated and does not need to be brushed with oil to stop food sticking to it, whereas greaseproof paper needs a light brushing with cooking oil.

USEFUL BAKING TINS

- 2 nonstick baking sheets
- 18 cm (7 inch) round deep cake tin
- 18 cm (7 inch) round, loose-bottomed, deep cake tin
- two 20 cm (8 inch) Victoria sandwich tins
- 20 cm (8 inch) round springform tin or loose-bottomed tin
- 20 cm (8 inch) fluted-edged, loose-bottomed flan tin
- 28 cm (11 inch) fluted-edged, loose-bottomed flan tin
- 18 cm (7 inch) square deep cake tin
- 20 cm (8 inch) square deep cake tin
- 20 cm (8 inch) square shallow cake tin
- 12-hole deep muffin tin
- 12-hole bun tray
- 1 kg (2 lb) loaf tin with a base measurement of 19 x 8 cm (7½ x 3½ inches) and 7.5 cm (3 inches) deep
- small roasting tin with a base measurement of 18 x 28 cm (7 x 11 inches) and about 4 cm (1½ inches) deep
- medium roasting tin with a base measurement of 30 x 23 cm (12 x 9 inches) and about 4 cm (1½ inches) deep

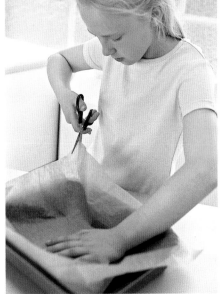

baking sheets

Brush baking sheets with a little cooking oil before use.

victoria sandwich tins

Brush the base and sides of the tins with a little oil then stand one of the tins on a double thickness piece of greaseproof paper. Draw around the tin, cut out the shape, then press a paper circle on to the base of each tin and brush the paper lightly with a little extra oil.

deep round or square tins

Deep tins can be base-lined in the same way as a sandwich tin or the sides may need lining, too, if the cake takes a long time to cook – see each recipe for details.

If lining the base and sides of the tin, first stand the tin on a piece of nonstick baking paper, rather than greaseproof paper. Draw around the tin then cut out the shape for the base. Next cut a strip of paper, a little higher than the cake tin sides and long enough to go all the way round the cake tin and overlap slightly. Fold up the bottom edge by about 1 cm (½ inch) then make small scissor cuts up to the fold line at intervals along the strip of paper for a round tin, or just at the corners for a square or rectangular-shaped tin. Arrange the paper strip around the inside of the tin so that the folded and snipped edge is at the bottom of the tin and the ends of the long strip overlap slightly. Place the paper base on top.

roasting tins

Cut a large piece of nonstick baking paper a little larger than the tin, make diagonal cuts into the corners of the paper then press into the tin, tucking the snipped edges one behind the other for a snug fit over the base and up the sides of the tin.

loaf tins

Brush the inside of the tin with a little oil then cut a strip of greaseproof paper the length of the longest side and wide enough to go over the base and up the two long sides of the tin. Press the paper into the tin and brush with a little extra oil.

Alternatively, line the loaf tin with a large piece of nonstick baking paper, snip into the corners of the paper as if lining a roasting tin then press into the tin (there is no need to oil the tin or the paper).

cake-making techniques

Cake-making really is not difficult. There are various different ways to make cakes. Once you get to know these basic techniques you should enjoy success every time and be able to impress your friends and family with your baking skills and tasty results!

rubbing in

This method is most often used for making scones, shortbread cookies and loaf cakes.

- Put the flour and sugar in a large bowl then cut the butter into small pieces and add to the bowl.
- Lift a little of the butter and flour out of the bowl and, with the palms of your hands facing upwards, rub the flour and fat across your fingers with your thumbs.
- Try to use butter or margarine that is at room temperature so that it will be easier for you to rub into pieces. If it is very hard when you take it out of the fridge, then soften (but don't melt) it for a few seconds in the microwave before you cut it into pieces.
- If you have a hand-held electric mixer or a food processor, you may like to use this instead of your fingertips.
- Stir in the required flavourings then mix with beaten eggs, milk or fruit juices, or for shortbread simply squeeze the crumbs together to make a dough.

melting

With this method, the cake – most often a gingerbread or flapjack – is made by melting together butter with sugar, golden syrup, honey or treacle, and then mixing this with dry ingredients such as flour, spices, nuts, seeds, oats and muesli.

- Use a medium or large saucepan so that there will be plenty of room to mix in the next ingredients.
- Stir the mixture while melting to make sure that all the butter has melted and the sugar has completely dissolved.
- Keep the heat low so that the mixture does not burn.
- Take the pan off the heat and mix in the dry ingredients.

creaming

This method involves creaming or beating together the fat and sugar and is most often used for large special cakes.

- First beat the butter (kept at room temperature, so that it is soft) or soft margarine and sugar together in a mixing bowl until light and fluffy, using either a wooden spoon or an electric mixer.
- Gradually mix in alternate spoonfuls of beaten egg and flour until the mixture is smooth. Do not add the eggs all at once or the mixture will separate or 'curdle'.

using eggs

Eggs are widely used in baking, either whole or separated into yolks and whites.

- To break open an egg, crack the shell by tapping its centre over the rim of the bowl.
- Hold the egg over the bowl, enlarge the crack with your fingers until the egg is almost in two halves.
- Tip the egg into the bowl and beat it with a fork until an even yellow. Discard the shell.

separating an egg

- Crack the egg as above but as you enlarge the crack and separate the shell, try to keep the yolk in one of the halves so that the white runs between the shells into the bowl.
- Gently tip the egg yolk into the other half shell so that any remaining egg white caught by the first shell half drops into the bowl, then tip the yolk into another bowl.
- If you drop a little egg yolk into the bowl of egg whites, don't worry, just scoop it out with a jagged piece of egg shell.

one-stage, or all-in-one cakes

This type of cake is perhaps the easiest of all cakes to make as all the ingredients are put into the bowl at the same time and mixed together.

All-in-one cakes are usually made with soft margarine, but butter that has been stored at room temperature or softened in the microwave for a few seconds can also be used. They often include a little baking powder as well as self-raising flour to make sure that they rise well.

whisking egg whites

- The secret to whisking egg whites is to use a bowl that is completely dry and clean, the whisk or beaters must also be clean and dry and there must be no egg yolk present. Any traces of butter or margarine will also stop the egg whites from whisking up.
- A hand-held electric whisk will whisk eggs quickly, but if you don't have one then use a balloon or rotary whisk and try to get a brother, sister or parent to share the work.
- As you use the whisk, you will see the clear egg whites turn to a frothy foam. As more air is trapped, it will become a thick white mixture that can be lifted into peaks.
- To check whether the egg whites are thick enough, tilt the bowl. If they slide, then whisk a little longer until you feel brave enough to turn the bowl upside down without them falling out!
- The egg whites can hold the trapped air for only a short while, so use them quickly before they have a chance to deflate.

using yeast

All the recipes in the bread chapter use fast-action dried yeast. Simply stir it into the flour, adding salt for flavour and a little sugar as food for the yeast, then activate the yeast with warm water or milk. Warmth is the key, so make sure that the water is warm enough to encourage the yeast to grow and multiply but not so hot that it kills it or so cold that it won't get the yeast started.

If you are not sure what kind of yeast you have then read the back of the pack carefully.

baking tips

Once your cake, cookies or bread are in the oven, you can start clearing up the kitchen, but don't forget your creation and leave it in the oven to burn! Unless the cake is to be served warm, like scones or muffins, let it cool completely before serving or storing it in an airtight container.

is my cake or bread cooked?

Always take great care when testing cakes, cookies and bread as they will be hot and the tins could easily burn your hands. Always use oven gloves and make sure an adult is there to help you if necessary.

cup cakes and sandwich cakes (1)

Press the top of the cake lightly with a fingertip – if the cake springs back it is ready. If a dent remains then put the cake back in the oven and check again at 5-minute intervals.

cookies

When cooked, cookies should be golden brown on top and still slightly soft underneath – they will harden on cooling.

large cakes (2)

Push a fine metal or wooden skewer into the centre of the cake then bring it out. If the skewer looks clean and dry, the cake is ready; if it is messy and sticky with cake mixture, the cake is not cooked through. Put it back in the oven and check again at 10- to 15-minute intervals.

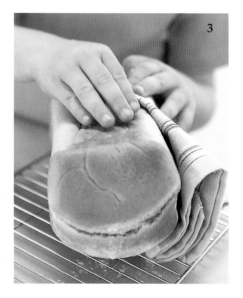

breads (3)

Tap the top or bottom with your fingertips – if it sounds hollow then it is ready. If you are unsure when making a large loaf then tap on the top, loosen and remove it from the tin then tap the base to double-check. If the base seems a little soft and damp then put the bread back in the oven without the tin, straight on to the oven shelf, and test again after 5 minutes.

what went wrong?

Sometimes things go wrong in cake-making. Don't be disheartened – just look at the suggestions below as to where you might have gone wrong, work out the problem and try the recipe again.

if the cake sank...

- Perhaps you kept opening the oven door during cooking.
- Did you take the cake out of the oven before it was fully cooked?
- Did you forget to use one of the ingredients?
- Perhaps you used too much baking powder. Did you use an accurate spoon measure, or an ordinary spoon from the cutlery drawer?

if the cake has not risen...

- The oven may have been at too low a temperature, or turned off accidentally.
- Perhaps you did not use enough baking powder or bicarbonate of soda.
- You may have used plain flour instead of self-raising.
- Perhaps the whisked-in air was knocked out when folding in egg whites (as for a cheesecake) or flour (as for a Swiss roll).

STORAGE

Once your cake or cookies have completely cooled put them in an airtight tin or plastic container and store in a cool place. For large cakes it can be helpful to put the cake on the lid then cover with the upside-down container so that it is easier to slice the cake while still in the container. Cakes with cream or cream cheese fillings or frosting need to be kept in the fridge.

if the cake has cracked and is too brown on top...

- The oven was probably too hot. (If using a fan-assisted oven, was the necessary adjustment made to the temperature?)
- The cake may have been cooked on too high an oven shelf.

if the fruit in the cake has sunk to the bottom...

- There may have been too much liquid in the cake. If large eggs were used instead of medium ones, the cake mixture may have been too wet to hold the fruit up.

cook's terms

baking
To cook food in the oven.

beating
To soften an ingredient or mix it with another ingredient, usually using a wooden spoon or a fork.

chopping (1)
To cut food into tiny pieces.

chunks
Pieces of food in larger pieces than diced food (see 'dicing').

creaming
To beat butter or margarine together with sugar using a wooden spoon or an electric mixer until light and fluffy and very smooth.

decorating
To finish off the top of a cake or cookies attractively.

dicing
To cut food into small cubes about the size of your fingernail.

draining
To pour off the liquid from food through a sieve or colander.

drizzling
To spoon wiggly scribble-like lines of icing or melted chocolate over the top of a baked cake or cookies, or to sprinkle a little oil over bread dough before baking.

folding in (2)
To mix ingredients together with a very gentle stirring action to keep the air in the mixture, for example when mixing in whipped cream for a filling, when folding in flour to a Swiss roll mixture or when folding whisked egg whites into a cheesecake mixture.

- Use a metal spoon such as a dessertspoon or serving spoon with a large bowl and gently stir the spoon through the two different mixtures in a figure of eight or swirling movement.
- Slowly turn the spoon so that the mixture on the bottom of the bowl is gently lifted and mixed with that on the top.

grating
To make tiny pieces, by rubbing an ingredient such as an orange, lemon, lime or block of cheese against a grater – a metal blade with small rough-edged holes pressed into it.

greasing (3)
To coat a cooking utensil such as a cake tin with a little cooking oil or softened butter or margarine, to prevent food sticking when cooked.

kneading (4)

To smooth the outside of a dough when making shortbread cookies, scones, pastry and bread.

- Sprinkle a little flour on to the work surface then tip the dough out on top. Fold half of the dough back on itself using your hands, then turn slightly and do this a few more times until the dough is smooth.
- Unlike shortbread or scones, bread that has yeast added needs a lot of kneading and can take quite rough treatment. Clench your fist and press into the dough to stretch it, then fold the dough back, turn it and repeat it for 5 minutes. Five minutes will seem like ages, so check with the clock so that you know what time you started. After a few minutes you will really begin to feel and see the difference and the more you knead, the less flour you will need on the work surface to stop the dough sticking.

lining (5)

To put greaseproof or nonstick baking paper into the base or the base and sides of a cake tin so that the cake does not stick to the tin when cooked (see page 12).

sieving

To remove the lumps from dry ingredients such as flour, cocoa powder, brown sugar and icing sugar by pressing or shaking them through the fine mesh of a sieve.

- Rest the handle and edges of the sieve over a mixing bowl.
- Add the ingredient to be sieved then press it through the holes of the sieve using the back of a metal spoon.

sifting

Another term for sieving ingredients (see 'sieving').

simmering

To cook liquid in a saucepan over a gentle heat so that bubbles just break the surface.

squeezing (6)

To press the juice from a lemon, lime or orange, using a lemon squeezer.

whisking

To beat air into ingredients such as egg whites, whole eggs and sugar, or cream (see 'whipping') using a balloon, rotary or electric whisk so that they become very thick.

whipping

Another term for whisking (see 'whisking'), usually mentioned only when using cream.

double berry muffins

makes
12

equipment

12 paper muffin cases

12-hole deep muffin tin

kitchen scales and
measuring spoons

large mixing bowl

fork

small saucepan or
microwave-proof bowl

2 dessertspoons

round-bladed knife

wire rack

ingredients

300 g (10 oz) plain flour

3 teaspoons baking
powder

125 g (4 oz) caster sugar

50 g (2 oz) butter

3 eggs

4 tablespoons sunflower
oil

1½ teaspoons vanilla
essence

150 g (5 oz) natural
yogurt

100 g (3½ oz) fresh
blueberries

100 g (3½ oz) fresh
raspberries

what to do

1 • Set the oven to 200°C/400°F/Gas Mark 6.

• Separate the paper muffin cases and put
one in each hole in the muffin tin.

2 • Put the flour, baking powder and sugar in
the mixing bowl and stir together using
the fork.

3 • Melt the butter in the saucepan on the
hob, or in the bowl in the microwave on
full power for 30 seconds.

• Pour the melted butter into the flour and
sugar mixture.

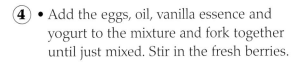

4 • Add the eggs, oil, vanilla essence and yogurt to the mixture and fork together until just mixed. Stir in the fresh berries.

5 • Divide the mixture between the paper cases using 2 spoons.

• Bake for 15 minutes until the muffins are well risen and the tops have cracked and turned golden brown. Loosen the edges of the paper cases with the round-bladed knife then transfer to the wire rack. Serve the muffins warm – they are best eaten on the day they are made.

banana and poppy seed muffins 🍎

makes
12

equipment

12 paper muffin cases

12-hole deep muffin tin

kitchen scales and
measuring spoons

large mixing bowl

small saucepan or
microwave-proof bowl

plate

fork

dessertspoon

round-bladed knife

wire rack

ingredients

250 g (8 oz) self-raising
flour

125 g (4 oz) caster sugar

2 tablespoons poppy
seeds (optional)

50 g (2 oz) butter

1 ripe banana,
about 150 g (5 oz)
before peeling

2 eggs

4 tablespoons natural
yogurt

what to do

1 • Set the oven to 200°C/400°F/Gas Mark 6.

  • Separate the paper muffin cases and put
    one in each hole in the muffin tin.

2 • Put the flour, sugar and poppy seeds, if
    using, in the mixing bowl.

3 • Melt the butter in the saucepan on the
    hob, or in the bowl in the microwave on
    full power for 30 seconds.

  • Peel then mash the banana on the plate
    using the fork.

4

4

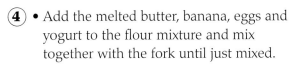

4 • Add the melted butter, banana, eggs and yogurt to the flour mixture and mix together with the fork until just mixed.

5 • Spoon the muffin mixture into the paper cases. Bake for 15 minutes until the muffins are well risen and golden brown.

• Loosen the edges of the paper cases with the round-bladed knife then transfer them to the wire rack to cool. Serve the muffins warm or cold – they are best eaten on the day they are made.

25

christmas muffins

④

makes
12

ingredients

300 g (10 oz) plain flour

3 teaspoons baking powder

1 teaspoon ground cinnamon

½ teaspoon ground ginger

125 g (4 oz) dark muscovado sugar

200 g (7 oz) luxury mixed dried fruit

75 g (3 oz) butter

3 eggs

150 ml (¼ pint) milk

To finish

3 tablespoons apricot jam

icing sugar, for dusting the work surface

250 g (8 oz) marzipan or ready-to-roll white icing

tubes of red, yellow and green writing icing

equipment

12 foil or paper muffin cases

12-hole muffin tin

kitchen scales, measuring spoons and jug

large mixing bowl

wooden spoon

small saucepan or microwave-proof bowl

fork

dessertspoon

round-bladed knife

wire rack

rolling pin

6 cm (2½ inch) round and star-shaped cookie cutter

what to do

1 • Set the oven to 200°C/400°F/Gas Mark 6.

• Separate the muffin cases and put one in each hole in the muffin tin.

2 • Put the flour, baking powder, spices, sugar and dried fruit in the mixing bowl and stir together.

• Melt the butter in the saucepan on the hob, or in the bowl in the microwave on full power for 1 minute.

• Mix the melted butter, eggs and milk together with the fork then add to the flour mixture and stir until just mixed.

④

3 • Spoon the mixture into the muffin cases. Bake for 15 minutes until the muffins are well risen and browned.

• Loosen the edges of the cases from the tin with the round-bladed knife then transfer to the wire rack.

4 • To decorate the muffins, spread a little jam over the top of each muffin.

• Sprinkle the work surface with a little icing sugar then knead the marzipan or ready-to-roll icing and roll out thinly.

• Stamp out circles or stars using the cookie cutter and press one on the top of each muffin. Reknead and roll out the trimmings and continue until all the muffins have been topped.

5 • Decorate the top of each cake with writing icing. Leave the icing to harden before serving the muffins – they are best eaten on the day they are made.

tip

★ If you are short of time then serve the muffins without the decoration.

cheesy corn muffins

makes 12

equipment

12 paper muffin cases

12-hole muffin tin

kitchen scales, measuring spoons and jug

grater

plate

large mixing bowl

dessertspoon

fork

round-bladed knife

wire rack

ingredients

100 g (3½ oz) mature Cheddar cheese

125 g (4 oz) quick-cook polenta grains (cornmeal)

175 g (6 oz) self-raising flour

2 teaspoons baking powder

150 ml (¼ pint) milk

2 eggs

2 teaspoons Dijon mustard

4 tablespoons sunflower oil

salt and pepper

butter, to serve

what to do

1 • Set the oven to 200°C/400°F/Gas Mark 6.

• Separate the paper muffin cases and put one in each hole in the muffin tin.

• Coarsely grate the cheese on to the plate.

(2) • Put the polenta, flour and baking powder in the mixing bowl. Stir in the cheese.

• Put the milk, eggs, mustard and oil in the measuring jug and add a little salt and pepper. Beat together using the fork.

• Add the milk mixture to the polenta mixture and stir until just mixed.

28

3 • Spoon the muffin mixture into the paper cases. Bake for 15 minutes until the muffins are well risen and golden brown.

• Loosen the edges of the paper cases with the round-bladed knife then transfer to the wire rack. Serve the muffins warm, broken and spread with butter – they are best eaten on the day they are made.

tip

★ If you don't have any polenta replace it with the same quantity of plain flour.

apricot and white chocolate rockies

makes 24

equipment

pastry brush

2 baking sheets

kitchen scales and measuring spoons

scissors

plastic bag

rolling pin

medium mixing bowl

round-bladed knife

plate

electric mixer (optional)

dessertspoon

teaspoon

palette knife

wire rack

ingredients

oil, for greasing

100 g (3½ oz) ready-to-eat dried apricots

100 g (3½ oz) white chocolate

250 g (8 oz) self-raising flour

125 g (4 oz) butter, at room temperature

75 g (3 oz) caster sugar

1 egg

2–3 tablespoons milk

what to do

1. • Set the oven to 180°C/350°F/Gas Mark 4.

   • Lightly brush the baking sheets with a little oil.

   • Snip the apricots into small pieces with the scissors.

   • Put the chocolate in the plastic bag. Break it into pieces with the rolling pin.

(1)

(3)

2 • Put the flour in the mixing bowl. Cut the butter into pieces on the plate then add to the flour. Rub the butter into the flour between your fingertips to make tiny crumbs, or use an electric mixer.

• Stir in the sugar, snipped apricots and broken chocolate.

• Add the egg then mix in enough milk to make a soft lumpy-looking mixture.

3 • Using the dessertspoon and teaspoon, scoop and drop 24 mounds of the mixture on to the oiled baking sheets, leaving a little space in between to allow them to spread during cooking.

• Bake for 12–15 minutes until the cookies are pale golden and just firm to the touch.

• Loosen the cookies with the palette knife then transfer to the wire rack to cool. Eat the cookies on the day they are made.

mini raspberry sandwich cakes

**makes
12**

equipment

pastry brush

12-hole deep muffin tin

scissors

greaseproof paper

kitchen scales and
measuring spoons

large mixing bowl

wooden spoon or
electric mixer

2 dessertspoons

teaspoon

round-bladed knife

wire rack

sharp knife

sieve (optional)

ingredients

oil, for greasing

175 g (6 oz) soft
margarine

175 g (6 oz) caster sugar

175 g (6 oz) self-raising
flour

3 eggs

To finish

4 tablespoons seedless
raspberry jam

some fresh raspberries,
to decorate

2 tablespoons caster
sugar or sifted icing
sugar

what to do

1 • Set the oven to 180°C/350°F/Gas Mark 4.

• Lightly brush the holes in the muffin tin
with a little oil, line the bases with small
circles of greaseproof paper and brush
these lightly with a little extra oil.

2 • Put all the cake ingredients into the large
mixing bowl and beat together with the
wooden spoon or the electric mixer
until smooth.

• Spoon the cake mixture into the holes in the muffin tin and smooth flat with the back of the teaspoon.

3 • Bake for 10–12 minutes until the cakes are well risen and golden, and the tops spring back when lightly pressed with a fingertip.

• Loosen the sides of the cakes with the round-bladed knife then transfer to the wire rack and leave to cool.

4 • Cut each cake in half then spread the lower halves with the jam. Replace the cake tops, add the raspberries and sprinkle with a little sugar. These cakes are best eaten on the day they are made.

apple scones

makes 8–10

ingredients

oil, for greasing

1 dessert apple

75 g (3 oz) butter

375 g (12 oz) self-raising flour, plus a little extra for dusting the work surface

1 teaspoon ground cinnamon

75 g (3 oz) caster sugar

1 egg, beaten

150 ml (¼ pint) milk, plus 2 tablespoons for glazing

To serve

blackberry jam

whipped or clotted cream

equipment

pastry brush

large baking sheet

small sharp knife

chopping board

vegetable peeler

kitchen scales, measuring spoons and jug

small saucepan

medium and small bowls

round-bladed knife

plate

electric mixer (optional)

large metal spoon

rolling pin

5.5 cm (2¼ inch) round cookie cutter

teaspoon

wire rack

what to do

1 • Set the oven to 200°C/400°F/Gas Mark 6.

• Brush the baking sheet with a little oil.

2 • Cut the apple into quarters, cut away the core then peel and dice.

• Heat 25 g (1 oz) of the butter in the saucepan, add the apple and cook gently, without a lid, for 5 minutes until softened.

3 • Put the flour, half the cinnamon and 50 g (2 oz) of the sugar in the medium bowl.

• Cut the remaining butter into small pieces on the plate then add to the flour mixture. Rub the butter into the flour mixture between your fingertips to make tiny crumbs, or use an electric mixer.

- Add the cooked apples and the egg to the flour mixture then slowly stir in enough milk to mix to a soft dough.

4 • Sprinkle the work surface with flour, tip out the dough and knead lightly until smooth.

- Roll out until about 2.5 cm (1 inch) thick. Using the cookie cutter, stamp out as many circles as you can and place them on the oiled baking sheet.

- Shape the trimmings into a ball then roll out again and cut more circles. Keep doing this until all the dough has been used up.

5 • Brush the tops of the scones with milk.

- Mix the remaining sugar and cinnamon together in the small bowl then sprinkle over the tops of the scones.

- Bake for 12–15 minutes until the scones are well risen and browned. Remove from the baking sheet and transfer to the wire rack. Serve the scones warm, split and filled with blackberry jam and clotted cream.

butterfly cakes

equipment

12 paper cake cases

12-hole bun tray

kitchen scales and measuring spoons

large and medium mixing bowls

wooden spoon or electric mixer

dessertspoon

teaspoon

small sharp knife

round-bladed knife

chopping board

ingredients

125 g (4 oz) soft margarine

125 g (4 oz) caster sugar

125 g (4 oz) self-raising flour

2 eggs

1 teaspoon vanilla essence

Frosting

75 g (3 oz) butter, at room temperature

150 g (5 oz) icing sugar

½ teaspoon vanilla essence

1–2 teaspoons milk

To finish

hundreds and thousands or sugar strands

tubes of different coloured icing

selection of sweets

strips of angelica

what to do

1 • Set the oven to 180°C/350°F/Gas Mark 4.

• Separate the paper cake cases and put one in each hole in the bun tray.

2 • Put all the cake ingredients in the large mixing bowl and beat with the wooden spoon or electric mixer until smooth.

• Spoon the cake mixture into the cases.

3 • Bake for 15–18 minutes until the cakes are well risen and golden brown, and the tops spring back when lightly pressed.

(5)

(5)

- Leave the cakes to cool in the tin.

4 • Meanwhile, make the frosting. Put the butter into the second bowl and gradually beat in the icing sugar (there is no need to sift it first), vanilla essence and milk to make a smooth soft frosting.

⑤ • Cut out a small circle of cake, about 2.5 cm (1 inch) in diameter, from the centre of each cake by pressing the tip of the teaspoon at a slight angle into the centre of the cake and twisting in much the same way as when using a pair of compasses.

- Fill the holes with most of the frosting.

- Cut the small cake circles in half to make 'butterfly wings', spread thinly with the remaining frosting and press some hundreds and thousands on top. Carefully stick these 'wings' on to the frosting on the tops of the cakes.

- Pipe on wing shapes with coloured tubes of icing. Add sweets to some wings.

- Cut strips of angelica for the butterfly antennae. Dot one end of each strip with frosting and sprinkle with hundreds and thousands. Press the other end into the frosting. The cakes can be stored in an airtight tin for up to 2 days.

meringues with lemon curd cream

makes 16

equipment

large baking sheet

nonstick baking paper

large and medium mixing bowls

electric whisk

kitchen scales

teaspoon

dessertspoon

round-bladed knife

12 paper cake cases

ingredients

3 egg whites

175 g (6 oz) caster sugar

150 ml (¼ pint) double cream

2 tablespoons lemon curd

sugar flowers, to decorate

what to do

1 • Set the oven to 110°C/225°F/Gas Mark ¼.

• Line the baking sheet with the nonstick baking paper.

2 • Put the egg whites in the large mixing bowl and whisk using the electric whisk until very stiff. To test whether they are ready, turn the bowl upside down – if the eggs look like they may slide out, whisk for a few minutes more.

• Gradually whisk in the sugar a teaspoonful at a time and continue whisking for 1–2 minutes more, even when all the sugar has been added, so that the meringue is very thick and glossy.

(2)

(3)

(3) • Drop heaped teaspoonfuls of the meringue on the prepared baking sheet.

• Bake the meringues for about 1 hour until they are firm and can be lifted easily off the paper. If they stick on the bottom, cook them for 15 minutes longer.

• Leave the meringues to cool on the paper.

(4) • Using the cleaned electric whisk, whip the cream in the medium bowl until it has just thickened and makes soft swirls. Take care not to overwhip or it will look like butter.

• Stir the lemon curd into the cream then use it to sandwich the meringues together in pairs. Arrange them in the paper cake cases and decorate with sugar flowers. The meringues are best eaten on the day they are made, although unfilled ones may be stored in an airtight tin for up to 5 days.

tip

★ If you don't like lemon curd then leave it out of the cream.

39

ricotta griddle cakes

makes
20

equipment

kitchen scales,
measuring spoons and
jug

large mixing bowl

balloon whisk

kitchen paper

griddle or heavy-based
nonstick frying pan

large spoon

palette knife

clean tea towel

ingredients

175 g (6 oz) self-raising
flour

½ teaspoon baking
powder

1 tablespoon caster sugar

250 g (8 oz) tub ricotta
cheese

3 eggs

200 ml (7 fl oz) milk

2 tablespoons sunflower
oil

butter and jam, to serve

what to do

(1) • Put the flour, baking powder and sugar in
the mixing bowl.

• Add the ricotta, the eggs and a little of the
milk and whisk together until smooth.
Gradually whisk in the remaining milk.

(2) • Pour the oil on to a folded piece of kitchen
paper then rub over the surface of the
griddle or heavy-based nonstick frying
pan and heat the pan.

• Drop spoonfuls of the mixture on to the
hot griddle or frying pan and cook for 3–4
minutes until bubbles form on the top and
the cakes are golden brown underneath.

(1)

(2)

(2)

- Loosen the cakes and turn them over using the palette knife. Cook the second side for 1–2 minutes until golden and the cakes are cooked through.

- Remove the cakes with the palette knife and keep them hot wrapped in a clean tea towel. Cook the remaining mixture, wiping the griddle or pan with the oiled kitchen paper between batches as needed.

3 • Serve the cakes while still hot, spread with butter and jam.

cookies

noah's ark cookies 👕

makes
20

equipment

kitchen scales

round-bladed knife

plate

large mixing bowl

electric mixer (optional)

nonstick baking paper

rolling pin

animal-shaped cookie cutters

palette knife

baking sheets

wire rack

ingredients

175 g (6 oz) butter, at room temperature

75 g (3 oz) caster sugar

275 g (9 oz) plain flour

To finish

tubes of different coloured writing icing

mini candy-coated chocolate sweets

what to do

1 • Set the oven to 180°C/350°F/Gas Mark 4.

• Cut the butter into small pieces on the plate then put in the bowl with the sugar and flour.

• Rub the butter into the flour mixture between your fingertips to make tiny crumbs, or use an electric mixer.

• Using your hands squeeze the cookie crumbs together to make a dough. Knead lightly then cut in half.

② • Place one of the pieces of cookie dough between 2 large sheets of nonstick baking paper then roll out thinly.

• Peel off the top piece of paper and stamp out animal shapes using a selection of different cookie cutters, making 2 of each animal shape.

②

②

3 • Carefully lift the cookie animals with the palette knife and place on the ungreased baking sheets.

• Add the cookie trimmings to the other half of the cookie dough and squeeze together back into a ball. Continue rolling and stamping out the mixture until it has all been shaped into animals.

4 • Bake the cookies for about 10 minutes until they are pale golden. Leave to cool on the baking sheets, or transfer to the wire rack if preferred.

⑤ • When the cookies are cold, let your imagination run riot as you add the animal markings, piping features with tubes of coloured icing and adding sweets for eyes.

• Set the cookies aside for 30 minutes for the icing to harden before serving. They can be stored in an airtight tin for up to 2 days.

tips

★ Rolling out cookie mixture can be tricky for small children, so rolling it between 2 sheets of nonstick baking paper helps to stop it sticking and breaking apart.

★ For chocolate-flavoured animals, use 15 g (½ oz) less flour, adding cocoa powder in its place.

shortbread spirals

makes 16

equipment

kitchen scales and measuring spoons

small mug

teaspoon

round-bladed knife

plate

2 mixing bowls

electric mixer (optional)

rolling pin

nonstick baking paper

large baking sheet

ingredients

2 tablespoons cocoa powder

1 tablespoon boiling water

200 g (7 oz) butter, at room temperature

300 g (10 oz) plain flour

100 g (3½ oz) caster sugar

1 teaspoon vanilla essence

what to do

1 • Set the oven to 160°C/325°F/Gas Mark 3.

• Put the cocoa powder into the mug and mix with the boiling water until smooth.

2 • Cut the butter into small pieces on the plate then put it in a mixing bowl with the flour and sugar. Rub the butter into the flour mixture with your fingertips to make tiny crumbs, or use an electric mixer.

3 • Spoon half the cookie mixture into the second bowl, add the cocoa paste to one and the vanilla essence to the other.

• Squeeze the crumbs and cocoa paste together with your hands until the crumbs begin to stick together and form an evenly coloured dough. Wash your hands and repeat with the remaining crumbs and the vanilla essence.

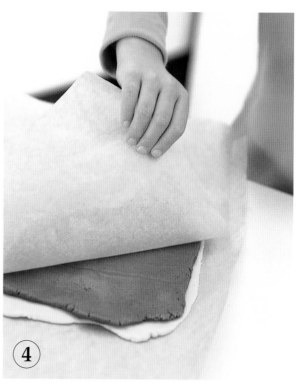

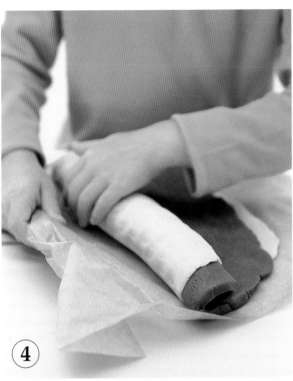

(4) • Roll out the cocoa dough between 2 sheets of nonstick baking paper to make a 20 cm (8 inch) square.

• Do the same with the vanilla dough, using another 2 sheets of nonstick baking paper.

• Peel the top sheets off each piece of dough. Put the cocoa dough on top of the vanilla dough so that the base paper you were rolling out on is now on top. Peel this off then roll up the double cookie mixture into a long roll, peeling away the other sheet of paper as you go. Chill for 15 minutes.

(5) • Cut the roll into 16 thick slices. Place on an ungreased baking sheet and cook for 8–10 minutes. Leave the cookies to cool on the baking sheet before serving.

peanut butter cookies

makes
20

equipment

pastry brush

2 baking sheets

kitchen scales and measuring spoons

plastic bag

rolling pin

large mixing bowl

wooden spoon or electric mixer

teaspoon

palette knife

wire rack

ingredients

oil, for greasing

75 g (3 oz) unsalted peanuts

75 g (3 oz) butter, at room temperature

75 g (3 oz) caster sugar

50 g (2 oz) light muscovado sugar

75 g (3 oz) crunchy peanut butter

150 g (5 oz) self-raising flour

1 egg

what to do

(1) • Set the oven to 180°C/350°F/Gas Mark 4.

• Lightly brush the baking sheets with a little oil.

• Put the peanuts in the plastic bag and hit with the rolling pin until broken into chunky pieces.

2 • Put the butter and white and brown sugar in the bowl, add the peanut butter and beat together with the wooden spoon or electric mixer until soft and fluffy.

- Add the flour, egg and two-thirds of the chopped nuts and stir together, squeezing with your hands when the mixture becomes too stiff to stir, until a soft dough is formed.

3 • Shape teaspoonfuls of the cookie mixture into 20 balls with your hands. Place on the oiled baking sheets, leaving a little space in between to allow them to spread during cooking.

- Press the remaining nuts on top of the cookies, then bake for 10–12 minutes until the cookies are golden brown.

4 • Leave to cool and harden on the baking sheets for 15 minutes then loosen with the palette knife and transfer to the wire rack to cool completely. The cookies can be stored in an airtight tin for up to 3 days.

makes
24

equipment

pastry brush

2 baking sheets

kitchen scales and
measuring spoons

large mixing bowl

wooden spoon or
electric mixer

grater

plate

teaspoon

small sharp knife

chopping board

palette knife

wire rack

melting 👝 moments

ingredients

oil, for greasing

125 g (4 oz) butter

125 g (4 oz) caster sugar

1 egg

grated rind of ½ orange

175 g (6 oz) self-raising flour

50 g (2 oz) rolled oats

6 glacé cherries

what to do

1 • Set the oven to 180°C/350°F/Gas Mark 4.

• Lightly brush the baking sheets with a little oil.

2 • Put the butter and sugar in the mixing bowl and beat with the wooden spoon or electric mixer until light and fluffy.

• Add the egg and orange rind then the flour. Mix until smooth.

3 • Put the oats on the plate.

• Shape teaspoonfuls of the cookie mixture into 24 balls with your hands then roll the balls in the oats.

• Put the cookies on the oiled baking sheets, leaving a little space for them to spread during cooking. Quarter the cherries and press a piece into each cookie.

③

③

4 • Bake the cookies for 12–15 minutes until they are lightly browned. Leave to cool and harden on the baking sheets for 15 minutes then transfer to the wire rack to cool completely. The cookies can be stored in an airtight tin for up to 3 days.

ruby fruit shorties

makes
18

equipment

kitchen scales and
measuring spoons

large mixing bowl

wooden spoon or
electric mixer

nonstick baking paper,
kitchen foil or clingfilm

round-bladed knife

baking sheet

wire rack

ingredients

150 g (5 oz) butter, at
room temperature

75 g (3 oz) light
muscovado sugar

50 g (2 oz) caster sugar

1 egg

1 teaspoon vanilla
essence

250 g (8 oz) plain flour

75 g (3 oz) mixed dried
blueberries and cherries

what to do

1 • Set the oven to 180°C/350°F/Gas Mark 4.

• Put the butter, white and brown and sugar
in the bowl and beat with the wooden
spoon or electric mixer until light and fluffy.

2 • Add the egg, vanilla essence and flour
and gently stir together until smooth.

• Mix in the dried fruits to make a smooth
soft dough.

• Spoon the cookie mixture into a line along
a piece of nonstick baking paper, kitchen
foil or clingfilm. Pat it into an even shape
about 30 cm (12 inches) long. Wrap it up.
Roll the cookie mixture backwards and
forwards to neaten the shape. Chill for at
least 15 minutes or up to 2 days.

3 • Unwrap and cut the mixture into 18 slices. Put them on an ungreased baking sheet and cook for 12–15 minutes until the cookies are a pale golden colour.

4 • Leave the cookies to cool for a few minutes then loosen them with the knife. Transfer them to the wire rack to cool completely. The cookies can be stored in an airtight tin for up to 3 days.

tip

★ Instead of the berries use sultanas, raisins, chopped dates, chopped dried apricots, chopped glacé cherries or a mixture of these, if you'd like.

iced stars

ingredients

2 egg whites

175 g (6 oz) icing sugar

½ teaspoon ground cinnamon

200 g (7 oz) ground almonds

2–3 teaspoons fresh lemon juice

oil, for greasing

30 g (1¼ oz) packet rainbow pearls

makes
25

equipment

large and small mixing bowls

electric whisk

kitchen scales and measuring spoons

teaspoon

tablespoon

clingfilm

lemon squeezer

pastry brush

2 baking sheets

rolling pin

nonstick baking paper

6 cm (2½ inch) star-shaped cookie cutter

round-bladed knife

what to do

1 • Put the egg whites into the large mixing bowl and whisk using the electric whisk until stiff and standing in peaks.

• Gradually whisk in the sugar a teaspoonful at a time. Add the cinnamon and whisk for 1–2 minutes more until the meringue is thick and glossy.

2 • Spoon 6 tablespoons of the meringue mixture into the smaller bowl, cover the bowl with clingfilm and set aside for later.

• Add the ground almonds to the large bowl of meringue and gently fold together. Gradually fold in enough lemon juice to make a thick paste.

• Cover the bowl with clingfilm and chill for 1 hour.

• Set the oven to 180°C/350°F/Gas Mark 4.

• Lightly brush the baking sheets with a little oil.

(3) • Roll out the almond dough between 2 large sheets of nonstick baking paper until it is about 5 mm (¼ inch) thick.

• Peel off the top piece of paper and stamp stars out of the dough using the cookie cutter. Carefully transfer the star-shaped cookies to the oiled baking sheets. Shape the trimmings into a ball and roll out on the paper. Stamp out more stars until all the cookie mixture has been used.

4 • Bake the cookies for about 5 minutes, changing the baking sheets over halfway through cooking, then remove the baking sheets from the oven and reduce the temperature to 110°C/225°F/Gas Mark ¼.

• Spoon a little of the reserved meringue on to each cookie then, using a pastry brush or the tip or a knife, ease the meringue all over the hot cookies.

• Press the rainbow pearls on to the star points. Return the cookies to the oven for 5 minutes until the meringue icing has dried out but not coloured.

• Loosen the cookies with a palette knife, then leave to cool. The cookies can be stored in an airtight tin for up to 5 days.

makes
10

equipment

kitchen scales and
measuring spoons

1 large and 2 small
mixing bowls

wooden spoon or
electric mixer

sieve

teaspoon

2 large baking sheets

fork

round-bladed knife

chocolate kisses

ingredients

100 g (3½ oz) butter, at
room temperature

50 g (2 oz) caster sugar

2 tablespoons cocoa
powder

150 g (5 oz) self-raising
flour

Filling

50 g (2 oz) butter, at
room temperature

100 g (3½ oz) icing sugar

a few drops peppermint
essence

a few drops green and
pink food colouring
(optional)

what to do

1 • Set the oven to 180°C/350°F/Gas Mark 4.

2 • Put the butter and sugar in the large bowl
and beat with the wooden spoon or
electric mixer until light and fluffy.

• Sift in the cocoa powder and flour and
mix together until smooth, squeezing with
your hands when the dough becomes too
stiff to stir.

(3) • Take teaspoonfuls of the dough, roll into
20 balls and put on the ungreased baking
sheets, leaving a little space in between to
allow them to spread during cooking.

- Flatten the cookies slightly with the back of the fork then bake for 10 minutes until they are lightly browned.

- Leave to cool on the baking sheets.

4 • Meanwhile, make the filling by beating together the butter, icing sugar and peppermint essence in one of the smaller bowls until smooth. Spoon half the filling into another bowl and, if you like, mix a few drops of green food colouring into one half and a little pink food colouring into the rest in the other bowl.

- Spread 5 of the cookies with the green filling and 5 with the pink then top with the remaining cookies. They can be stored in an airtight tin for up to 2 days.

tip

★ If you are short of time serve the cookies without the filling.

★ If you are not a fan of peppermint leave it out of the filling or add a little grated orange rind instead.

chunky chocolate and oat cookies 🎽

makes
20

equipment

pastry brush

2 baking sheets

kitchen scales and
measuring spoons

plastic bag

rolling pin

mixing bowl

wooden spoon or
electric mixer

teaspoon

palette knife

wire rack

ingredients

oil, for greasing

100 g (3½ oz) white
chocolate

100 g (3½ oz) dark
chocolate

125 g (4 oz) butter, at
room temperature

125 g (4 oz) light
muscovado sugar

1 egg, beaten

125 g (4 oz) wholemeal
self-raising flour

1 tablespoon cocoa
powder

50 g (2 oz) porridge oats

what to do

1 • Set the oven to 180°C/350°F/Gas Mark 4.

• Brush the baking sheets with a little oil.

• Put all the chocolate into the plastic bag
and hit with the rolling pin until broken
into roughly shaped pieces.

② • Put the butter and sugar in the mixing
bowl and beat with the wooden spoon
or electric mixer until light and fluffy.

②

②

- Add the egg, flour, cocoa powder and oats and mix until smooth.

- Stir in the chocolate pieces.

(3) • Scoop heaped teaspoons of the mixture on to the oiled baking sheets, leaving a little space in between to allow them to spread during cooking.

- Bake the cookies for 10–13 minutes until they are lightly browned. Leave to harden for 1–2 minutes then loosen with the palette knife and transfer to the wire rack to cool completely. The cookies are best eaten on the day they are made.

sweetheart cookies

makes 15

ingredients

oil, for greasing

200 g (7 oz) plain flour, plus a little extra for dusting the work surface

25 g (1 oz) custard powder

50 g (2 oz) caster sugar

150 g (5 oz) butter, at room temperature

1 egg yolk

4 tablespoons seedless raspberry jam

sifted icing sugar, to decorate

equipment

pastry brush

2 baking sheets

kitchen scales and measuring spoons

large mixing bowl

round-bladed knife

plate

electric mixer (optional)

rolling pin

6 cm (2½ inch) fluted round cookie cutter

3 cm (1¼ inch) heart-shaped cookie cutter

small sharp knife

palette knife

small sieve

what to do

1 • Set the oven to 160°C/325°F/Gas Mark 3.

   • Lightly brush the baking sheets with a little oil.

2 • Put the flour, custard powder and sugar in the bowl. Cut the butter into pieces on the plate then add to the bowl. Rub the butter into the flour mixture between your fingertips to make tiny crumbs, or use an electric mixer.

3 • Stir in the egg yolk and mix to a smooth dough, first with the round-bladed knife then with your hands when the dough becomes too stiff to stir.

4 • Knead the dough on a surface sprinkled with a little flour then cut it in half and roll out one half until about 5 mm (¼ inch) thick. Stamp out large circles using the round cookie cutter.

• Cut out little hearts from the centre of half the circles, using the heart-shaped cutter, and lift out with the end of the small sharp knife. Transfer the rounds to the oiled baking sheets.

• Squeeze the trimmings together and roll out with the remaining dough, stamping out shapes until you have 15 circles with heart-shaped centres cut out and 15 whole circles.

5 • Bake the cookies for 10–12 minutes – slightly less for the heart-stamped ones – until they are pale golden. Loosen the cookies with the palette knife and leave to cool on the baking sheets. They can be stored in an airtight tin for up to 2 days.

6 • To serve, spread the jam over the whole cookies, top with the heart-stamped ones then dust with a little sifted icing sugar.

tip

★ If you don't have a small heart-shaped cutter, use the upturned end of a piping nozzle to cut out tiny circles instead.

muesli 👕 munchies

(2)

makes
24

ingredients

oil, for greasing

125 g (4 oz) butter, at room temperature

125 g (4 oz) light muscovado sugar

1 egg

150 g (5 oz) self-raising flour

75 g (3 oz) ready-to-eat dried apricots

75 g (3 oz) 'no-added sugar' muesli

jumbo oats, to decorate (optional)

equipment

pastry brush

2 baking sheets

kitchen scales and measuring spoons

large mixing bowl

wooden spoon or electric mixer

scissors

teaspoon

palette knife

wire rack

what to do

1 • Set the oven to 180°C/350°F/Gas Mark 4.

• Brush the baking sheets with a little oil.

(2) • Put the butter and sugar in the mixing bowl and beat with the wooden spoon or electric mixer until light and fluffy.

• Add the egg and flour and beat until smooth.

• Snip the apricots into small pieces with scissors then mix into the cookie mixture with the muesli.

(3) • Spoon heaped teaspoonfuls of the mixture on to the oiled baking sheets, leaving a little space in between to allow them to spread during cooking.

(2)

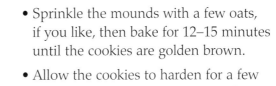

- Sprinkle the mounds with a few oats, if you like, then bake for 12–15 minutes until the cookies are golden brown.

- Allow the cookies to harden for a few minutes, then loosen them with the palette knife and transfer to the wire rack to cool completely. They can be stored in an airtight tin for up to 2 days.

tip

★ If you don't have any apricots, then add the same weight of chopped glacé cherries, or whole sultanas or raisins.

banana, fig and cranberry slice

(3)

cuts into 10 slices

equipment

pastry brush

1 kg (2 lb) loaf tin (see page 12)

scissors

greaseproof paper

kitchen scales and measuring spoons

plate

lemon squeezer

fork

large mixing bowl

wooden spoon

dessertspoon

skewer

round-bladed knife

wire rack

ingredients

oil, for greasing

3 small bananas, about 400 g (13 oz)

1 tablespoon lemon juice

125 g (4 oz) butter, at room temperature

150 g (5 oz) light muscovado sugar

2 eggs

175 g (6 oz) self-raising flour

125 g (4 oz) wholemeal self-raising flour

125 g (4 oz) dried figs

75 g (3 oz) dried cranberries

2 tablespoons sunflower seeds

what to do

1 • Set the oven to 180°C/350°F/Gas Mark 4.

• Brush the loaf tin with a little oil, then cut a piece of greaseproof paper to cover the base and up the 2 longest sides. Place in the tin and brush with a little extra oil.

2 • Peel the bananas then mash them on the plate with the lemon juice, using the fork.

(3)

62

(4)

(3) • Put the butter and sugar in the mixing bowl and beat with the wooden spoon until light and fluffy.

• Add the mashed banana, eggs and flours and beat together until smooth.

• Snip the figs into small pieces with scissors then add to the banana mixture with the cranberries and stir together.

(4) • Spoon the mixture into the tin, smooth flat and sprinkle with the sunflower seeds.

• Bake for 1 hour until the cake is well risen and golden brown, the top has cracked slightly, and a skewer comes out cleanly.

• Leave the cake to cool in the tin for 30 minutes, then loosen the sides with the round-bladed knife and turn it out on to the wire rack. Remove the lining paper and leave to cool. Cut into thick slices to serve.

malted gingerbread squares

makes
16

equipment

pastry brush

20 cm (8 inch) square
deep cake tin

scissors

greaseproof paper

kitchen scales,
measuring spoons
and jug

medium saucepan

wooden spoon

fork

mixing bowl

skewer

round-bladed knife

wire rack

ingredients

oil, for greasing

125 g (4 oz) butter

125 g (4 oz) dark
muscovado sugar

125 g (4 oz) barley malt
extract

125 g (4 oz) golden
syrup

150 ml (¼ pint) semi-
skimmed milk

2 eggs

150 g (5 oz) self-raising
flour

150 g (5 oz) wholemeal
plain or Granary flour

1 teaspoon bicarbonate
of soda

4 teaspoons ground
ginger

rye flakes or jumbo
porridge oats, for
sprinkling (optional)

what to do

1 • Set the oven to 180°C/350°F/Gas Mark 4.

    • Lightly brush the tin with a little oil, line
the base with greaseproof paper and
brush this lightly with a little extra oil.

② • Put the butter, sugar, malt extract and
syrup into the saucepan and heat gently,
stirring from time to time with the
wooden spoon until the butter has
melted, then take off the heat.

- Beat the milk and eggs in the jug using the fork.

- Mix all the dry ingredients in the bowl.

(3) • Add the dry ingredients to the saucepan. Beat until smooth. Add the milk mixture, little by little, and beat until smooth.

4 • Pour the mixture into the lined tin. Sprinkle with a few rye flakes or oats, if you like, and bake for 35–40 minutes until the cake is well risen and deep brown, and a skewer comes out cleanly when pushed into the centre of the cake.

- Leave the cake to cool in the tin for 30 minutes, then loosen the sides with the round-bladed knife and turn out on to the wire rack. Remove the lining paper and leave to cool completely. Cut into 16 squares to serve. The gingerbread can be stored in an airtight tin for up to 1 week.

coconut, cherry and lime cake

(3)

cuts into
15—18 slices

equipment

pastry brush

18 cm (7 inch) square
deep cake tin

scissors

greaseproof paper

kitchen scales and
measuring spoons

large, medium and small
mixing bowls

wooden spoon

sieve

kitchen paper

small sharp knife

chopping board

grater

skewer

round-bladed knife

wire rack

ingredients

oil, for greasing

200 g (7 oz) butter, at
room temperature

200 g (7 oz) caster sugar

4 eggs

250 g (8 oz) self-raising
flour

200 g (7 oz) glacé
cherries

75 g (3 oz) desiccated
coconut

grated rind of 2 limes

To finish

75 g (3 oz) glacé cherries

150 g (5 oz) icing sugar

squeezed juice of 1 lime

2 tablespoons desiccated
coconut

what to do

1 • Set the oven to 180°C/350°F/Gas Mark 4.

• Brush the tin with a little oil, line the base
with a square of greaseproof paper and
brush this lightly with a little extra oil.

2 • Put the butter and sugar into the large
mixing bowl and beat with the wooden
spoon until light and fluffy.

• Put the eggs in the medium bowl and
beat with the fork. Add alternate
spoonfuls of egg and then flour to the

(3)

butter mixture and keep adding and beating until everything has been added.

(3) • Put the cherries in a sieve, rinse under the cold tap then pat dry with kitchen paper. Cut them into quarters on the chopping board then put them in the small bowl and toss with the coconut and lime rind.

• Add to the ingredients in the large mixing bowl and stir together gently.

4 • Spoon the mixture into the lined tin and smooth flat with the back of the wooden spoon.

• Bake the cake for 45–55 minutes until it is well risen and golden brown, and a skewer comes out cleanly when pushed into the centre of the cake.

• Leave the cake to cool in the tin for 10 minutes, then loosen the sides with the round-bladed knife and turn out on to the wire rack. Remove the lining paper and leave to cool completely.

(5) • To decorate, cut the cherries into halves. Sift the icing sugar into the washed medium bowl then gradually mix in enough lime juice to make a smooth icing.

• Spoon the icing on to the top of the cake and spread with the back of the spoon so that a little runs down the sides.

• Arrange the halved cherries on top of the cake in a heart shape and sprinkle the cake with the coconut. Leave for 30 minutes for the icing to harden. Cut the cake into slices to serve.

cuts into
8 slices

equipment

pastry brush

18 cm (7 inch) round
deep cake tin

scissors

greaseproof paper

sieve

1 large and 2 small bowls

chopping board

kitchen paper

small sharp knife

kitchen scales and
measuring spoons

wooden spoon

fork

dessertspoon

skewer

round-bladed knife

wire rack

tropical fruit cake

ingredients

oil, for greasing

220 g (7½ oz) can sliced
pineapple

250 g (8 oz) dried ready-
to-eat exotic fruits

75 g (3 oz) glacé cherries

175 g (6 oz) butter, at
room temperature

175 g (6 oz) caster sugar

3 eggs

250 g (8 oz) plain flour

50 g (2 oz) desiccated
coconut

what to do

1 • Set the oven to 160°C/325°F/Gas Mark 3.

• Lightly brush the tin with a little oil, line
the base with a circle of greaseproof paper
and brush this lightly with a little extra oil.

• Tip the canned pineapple into the sieve
set over a small bowl and drain well. Tip
out on to the chopping board, pat dry
with a piece of kitchen paper then cut
into small pieces.

• Cut or snip the exotic fruits and the
cherries into pieces using the sharp knife
or scissors.

2 • Put the butter and sugar in the large
mixing bowl and beat with the wooden
spoon until light and fluffy.

- Put the eggs in a small bowl and beat with the fork.

- Gradually mix a spoonful of beaten egg then a spoonful of flour into the butter mixture and keep adding and mixing until both have been added and the mixture is smooth.

3 • Stir in the pineapple and exotic fruits then the glacé cherries and coconut.

- Spoon the mixture into the lined tin and smooth flat with the back of the spoon.

4 • Cook the cake for about 1–1¼ hours until it is golden brown, and a skewer comes out cleanly when pushed into the centre of the cake. Cover loosely with foil after 40 minutes if needed.

- Leave the cake to cool in the tin for 10 minutes, then loosen the sides with the round-bladed knife and turn out on to the wire rack. Remove the lining paper and leave to cool completely. Cut into slices to serve. The cake can be stored in an airtight tin for up to 1 week.

apple and madeira cake

cuts into
8–10 slices

ingredients

2 dessert apples

1 orange

175 g (6 oz) soft
margarine

175 g (6 oz) caster sugar

3 eggs

275 g (9 oz) self-raising
flour

little caster sugar,
to decorate

equipment

20 cm (8 inch) deep
round cake tin

nonstick baking paper

scissors

vegetable peeler

small knife

chopping board

grater

kitchen scales

large and small mixing
bowls

wooden spoon or
electric mixer

fork

skewer

what to do

1. • Set the oven to 160°C/325°F/Gas Mark 3.

   • Line the base and sides of the cake tin
   with nonstick baking paper (see page 12).

   • Peel the apples, cut them into quarters,
   then cut away the cores. Cut the apples
   into small pieces.

   • Finely grate the orange, then cut two slices
   and cut each one in half. (Eat the rest of
   the orange.)

2. • Put the margarine and sugar in the large
   mixing bowl and beat with the wooden
   spoon or electric mixer until light and fluffy.

- Put the eggs into the small bowl and mix together with a fork.

- Add a spoonful of egg then a spoonful of flour to the margarine mixture and mix until smooth. Continue adding alternate spoonfuls until both have been added and the mixture is smooth.

3 • Stir the apple pieces and grated orange rind into the cake mixture.

- Spoon the mixture into the lined tin and spread the top flat with the back of the spoon.

- Arrange the halved orange slices in the centre to make a pattern.

- Bake the cake for about 1 hour until it is well risen and golden brown and a skewer comes out cleanly when pushed into the centre of the cake.

4 • Carefully take the cake out of the tin and put it on the wire rack. Remove the lining paper and leave to cool completely.

- Sprinkle with a little extra sugar, then cut into slices to serve. The cake can be stored in an airtight tin for up to 1 week.

cuts into
10 slices

equipment

kitchen scales,
measuring spoons
and jug

small saucepan

medium mixing bowl

pastry brush

1 kg (2 lb) loaf tin
(see page 12)

scissors

greaseproof paper

grater

wooden spoon

dessertspoon

skewer

round-bladed knife

wire rack

apple and sultana loaf

ingredients

300 ml (½ pint) apple
juice

300 g (10 oz) sultanas

oil, for greasing

2 crisp dessert apples
(such as Granny Smith)

2 tablespoons chopped
mixed peel

125 g (4 oz) caster sugar

300 g (10 oz) self-raising
flour

1 egg

1 large piece citron peel,
to decorate (optional)

what to do

(1) • Pour the apple juice into the pan and bring
to the boil. Put the sultanas in the mixing
bowl then pour over the hot apple juice.

• Leave to soak for 4 hours or overnight.

2 • Set the oven to 160°C/325°F/Gas Mark 3.

• Brush the loaf tin with a little oil. Cut a
piece of greaseproof paper to fit over the
base and up the 2 longest sides. Place in
the tin and brush with a little extra oil.

(3) • Coarsely grate the apples down to the
cores then add the apple to the sultanas.

• Add the chopped peel, sugar, flour and
egg to the sultanas and mix with the
wooden spoon.

tip

★ Citron peel is a mix of candied orange, lime and lemon peel. The pieces are quarter sections of the whole fruit rind. It is not the same as chopped mixed peel.

- Spoon into the lined tin and smooth flat with the back of the metal spoon.

4 • Decorate the top of the cake with snipped strips of citron peel, if using.

- Bake the cake for about 1¼ hours until it is well risen and golden brown, and a skewer pushed into the centre comes out cleanly. Loosely cover it with foil if it is browning too fast.

5 • Leave the cake to cool in the tin for 30 minutes, then loosen the sides with the round-bladed knife and turn out on to the wire rack. Remove the lining paper and leave to cool completely.

- Cut into thick slices to serve. The loaf can be stored in an airtight tin for up to 3 days.

cuts into
10 slices

equipment

pastry brush

1 kg (2 lb) loaf tin
(see page 12)

scissors

greaseproof paper

grater

lemon squeezer

kitchen scales and
measuring spoons

small saucepan

large mixing bowl

wooden spoon or
electric mixer

dessertspoon

round-bladed knife

skewer

kitchen foil

wire rack

rippled date and orange loaf

ingredients

oil, for greasing

1 orange

250 g (8 oz) ready-
chopped stoned dates

6 tablespoons water

250 g (8 oz) self-raising
flour

½ teaspoon baking
powder

150 g (5 oz) caster sugar

150 g (5 oz) soft
margarine

3 eggs

what to do

(1) • Set the oven to 180°C/350°F/Gas Mark 4.

 • Lightly brush the loaf tin with a little oil,
   then cut a piece of greaseproof paper long
   enough to go over the base and up the
   2 longest sides. Place in the tin and brush
   lightly with a little extra oil.

 • Finely grate the rind from the orange.
   Cut it in half then squeeze the juice.

2 • Put the orange juice, dates and water in
   the saucepan and heat gently without a
   lid for 5 minutes until the dates are soft.

 • Leave to cool for 10 minutes.

(1)

(3)

the round-bladed knife and turn out on to the wire rack. Remove the lining paper and leave to cool before cutting into slices to serve. The cake can be stored in an airtight tin for up to 3 days.

(3) • Put the orange rind in the mixing bowl. Add all the remaining ingredients except the date mixture. Beat with the wooden spoon or electric mixer until smooth.

• Spoon one-third of the cake mixture into the lined tin and smooth flat with the back of the metal spoon.

• Dot half the date mixture over the cake mixture then smooth flat with the knife.

• Repeat one more time then cover with the last of the cake mixture.

4 • Bake for about 1 hour until the cake is well risen, cracked on top and golden brown. A skewer pushed into the centre should come out cleanly. Look at the cake after 30–40 minutes; loosely cover it with foil if it is browning too fast.

• Carefully loosen the sides of the cake with

farmhouse fruit cake

cuts into
8 slices

equipment

scissors

nonstick baking paper

18 cm (7 inch) round
deep cake tin

kitchen scales and
measuring spoons

1 large and 2 small
mixing bowls

wooden spoon or
electric mixer

fork

dessertspoon

small sharp knife

chopping board

skewer

kitchen foil

round-bladed knife

wire rack

ingredients

125 g (4 oz) butter, at
room temperature

125 g (4 oz) light
muscovado sugar

2 eggs

175 g (6 oz) self-raising
flour

½ teaspoon ground
cinnamon

a little grated nutmeg

250 g (8 oz) luxury
mixed dried fruit

To decorate

4 glacé cherries

1 large piece citron peel
(see 'Tip', page 73)

what to do

1 • Set the oven to 160°C/325°F/Gas Mark 3.

• Line the base and sides of the cake tin
with nonstick baking paper (see page 12).

2 • Put the butter and sugar in the large
mixing bowl and beat with the wooden
spoon or electric mixer until smooth.

• Beat the eggs in a smaller bowl with the
fork and mix the flour and spices in the
other small bowl.

• Gradually mix alternate spoonfuls of egg
and flour into the butter mixture until
both have been added and the mixture
is smooth.

• Stir in the dried fruit.

(2)

(3)

3 • Spoon the mixture into the lined tin and smooth flat with the back of the spoon.

• Cut the cherries in half and the citron peel into triangles, then arrange over the top of the cake.

• Bake the cake for about 1¼ hours or until it is well risen and browned, and a skewer comes out cleanly when pushed into the centre of the cake.

4 • Leave the cake to cool in the tin for 30 minutes, then loosen the sides with the round-bladed knife and turn out on to the wire rack. Remove the lining paper and leave to cool completely. The cake can be stored in an airtight tin for up to 1 week.

tip

★ Check on the cake from time to time during cooking and cover it loosely with kitchen foil if the top seems to be browning too quickly.

sesame and maple syrup flapjacks

equipment

scissors

nonstick baking paper

20 cm (8 inch) square shallow cake tin

kitchen scales and measuring spoons

medium saucepan

wooden spoon

dessertspoon

round-bladed knife

chopping board

large sharp knife

ingredients

200 g (7 oz) butter

200 g (7 oz) soft light brown sugar

5 tablespoons maple syrup or golden syrup

50 g (2 oz) sesame seeds, plus 1 extra tablespoon for sprinkling

250 g (8 oz) oats

what to do

1 • Set the oven to 180°C/350°F/Gas Mark 4.

 • Cut a square of nonstick baking paper a little larger than the tin, then snip into the corners and press the paper into the tin.

2 • Put the butter, sugar and syrup in the saucepan and heat gently, stirring from time to time with the wooden spoon, until completely melted.

3 • Take the saucepan off the heat and stir in the sesame seeds and oats.

 • Spoon the mixture into the lined tin and press flat with the back of the metal spoon.

• Sprinkle with the extra 1 tablespoon of sesame seeds.

4 • Bake the flapjack for 20–25 minutes until it is golden brown and just beginning to darken around the edges of the tin. Leave to cool for 10 minutes.

• Mark the flapjack into squares with the round-bladed knife and leave to harden and cool completely.

5 • Lift the paper and flapjack out of the tin, peel off the paper and put the flapjack on the chopping board. Cut into 9 pieces to serve. The flapjacks can be stored in an airtight tin for up to 3 days.

makes
18

triple choc brownies

(3)

equipment

scissors

nonstick baking paper

small roasting tin
(see page 12)

medium saucepan

large and medium
mixing bowls

kitchen scales and
measuring spoons

round-bladed knife

plate

plastic bag

rolling pin

electric whisk

large metal spoon

sieve

chopping board

large sharp knife

ingredients

150 g (5 oz) dark
chocolate

125 g (4 oz) butter, at
room temperature

75 g (3 oz) white
chocolate

75 g (3 oz) milk
chocolate

3 eggs

200 g (7 oz) caster sugar

150 g (5 oz) self-raising
flour

1 teaspoon baking
powder

what to do

1 • Set the oven to 180°C/350°F/Gas Mark 4.

• Cut a piece of nonstick baking paper a
little larger than the tin, then snip into the
corners and press the paper into the tin.

2 • Half-fill the saucepan with water, bring
just to the boil then turn off the heat and
place the large bowl on top.

• Break the dark chocolate into pieces and
cut the butter into pieces on the plate,
then add both to the large bowl. Leave for
5 minutes or so until melted.

(3) • Put the white and milk chocolate in the
plastic bag and hit with the rolling pin
until broken into small pieces.

(5)

4 • Whisk the eggs and sugar in the second bowl for 5 minutes using the electric whisk until thick and very frothy.

5 • Pour the melted chocolate and butter mixture over the top and mix in very gently using the metal spoon.

• Sift the flour and baking powder over the top then carefully fold in.

6 • Pour the mixture into the lined tin. Sprinkle the white and milk chocolate pieces over the top.

• Bake the cake for 20–25 minutes until the top is crusty and the centre still wobbles slightly. Leave to cool and harden in the tin.

7 • Lift the paper and cake out of the tin, remove the paper and put the cake on the chopping board. Cut into 18 pieces. The brownies can be stored in an airtight tin for up to 2 days.

tip

★ Melt the white chocolate and drizzle it from a spoon over the top of the cooked brownies instead of adding it to the raw mixture, if you prefer.

toffee apple squares

③

makes
15

ingredients

oil, for greasing

175 g (6 oz) soft
margarine

175 g (6 oz) light
muscovado sugar, plus 2
tablespoons for sprinkling

3 eggs

250 g (8 oz) self-raising
flour

1 teaspoon vanilla
essence

125 g (4 oz) hard
toffees, unwrapped

3 dessert apples

50 g (2 oz) butter

equipment

pastry brush

small roasting tin
(see page 12)

scissors

greaseproof paper

kitchen scales and
measuring spoons

large and small bowls

wooden spoon

fork

plastic bag

rolling pin

large and small knife

chopping board

vegetable peeler

dessertspoon

small saucepan

skewer and wire rack

what to do

1 • Set the oven to 180°C/350°F/Gas Mark 4.

• Brush the tin with a little oil. Cut a piece
of greaseproof paper to fit over the base
and partway up the 2 longest sides. Place
in the tin and brush with a little extra oil.

2 • Put the margarine and sugar in the large
bowl and beat with the wooden spoon
until smooth.

• Put the eggs in the small bowl and beat
with the fork. Gradually beat a little of
the eggs then a little of the flour into
the margarine mixture and keep adding
and beating until both have been added
and the mixture is smooth. Stir in the
vanilla essence.

③

3 • Put the toffees in the plastic bag and hit with the rolling pin until broken into chunky pieces.

• Quarter, core and peel the apples. Cut 4 quarters into small pieces and thinly slice the rest.

• Stir half the toffees and the small pieces of apple into the cake mixture then spoon into the lined tin and smooth flat.

• Arrange the apple slices neatly in rows over the top.

• Melt the butter in the saucepan on the hob. Brush the melted butter over the top of the apples, sprinkle with the rest of the toffees and the extra 2 tablespoons of the sugar.

4 • Bake the cake for 40–45 minutes until it is well risen and golden brown, and a skewer comes out cleanly when pushed into the centre of the cake.

• Leave the cake to cool in the tin then lift on to the wire rack. Peel off the paper and cut into 15 squares. Serve warm or cold. The squares can be stored in an airtight tin for up to 2 days.

makes
12

equipment

scissors

nonstick baking paper

20 cm (8 in) square
shallow cake tin

small sharp knife

chopping board

vegetable peeler

kitchen scales and
measuring spoons

small and medium
saucepans

wooden spoon

dessertspoon

round-bladed knife

large sharp knife

date and apple flapjack bars

ingredients

1 dessert apple

150 g (5 oz) ready–
chopped stoned dates

4 tablespoons water

150 g (5 oz) butter

75 g (3 oz) light
muscovado sugar

3 tablespoons golden
syrup

75 g (3 oz) wholemeal
plain or Granary flour

200 g (7 oz) 'no-added
sugar' muesli

3 tablespoons sunflower
seeds

3 tablespoons pine nuts
or roughly chopped
almonds or hazelnuts

what to do

1 • Set the oven to 180°C/350°F/Gas Mark 4.

   • Cut a square of nonstick baking paper a
   little larger than the tin, then snip into the
   corners and press the paper into the tin.

2 • Quarter, core and peel the apple then cut
   into small pieces.

④

④

- Put the apple and dates in the small saucepan with the water, cover and cook gently for 5 minutes until softened.

3 • Put the butter, sugar and golden syrup into the medium saucepan and heat gently, stirring from time to time with the wooden spoon until the butter has melted and the sugar has dissolved.

- Take the pan off the heat and stir in the flour, muesli, sunflower seeds and nuts.

④ • Spoon three-quarters of the mixture into the lined tin and press flat with the back of the metal spoon.

- Spoon the date mixture on top, draining off any remaining water.

- Top with spoonfuls of the remaining muesli mixture – don't worry if the date mixture shows through in places.

5 • Bake the flapjack for 25–30 minutes until it is a mid-brown colour. Leave to cool and harden for 10 minutes then mark into 12 bars. Leave the flapjack in the tin to cool completely.

- Lift the paper and flapjack out of the tin, peel off the paper and cut into bars on the chopping board. The flapjacks can be stored in an airtight tin for up to 3 days.

squashed fly bars

makes 16

equipment

pastry brush

small roasting tin
(see page 12)

scissors

greaseproof paper

kitchen scales

large mixing bowl

wooden spoon or
electric mixer

dessertspoon

round-bladed knife

wire rack

sieve

large sharp knife

ingredients

oil, for greasing

250 g (8 oz) soft
margarine

250 g (8 oz) caster sugar

250 g (8 oz) self-raising
flour

4 eggs

150 g (5 oz) sultanas

sifted icing sugar, to
decorate

what to do

1 • Set the oven to 180°C/350°F/Gas Mark 4.

• Brush the tin with a little oil. Cut a piece
of greaseproof paper to fit over the base
and partway up the 2 longest sides. Place
in the tin and brush with a little extra oil.

② • Put the margarine, sugar, flour and eggs
in the mixing bowl and beat with the
wooden spoon or electric mixer for
1–2 minutes until smooth.

• Stir in the sultanas.

③ • Pour the mixture into the lined tin and
smooth flat with the metal spoon.

• Bake the cake for 25–30 minutes until it
is well risen and golden brown, and the
top springs back when lightly pressed
with a fingertip.

4 • Leave the cake to cool in the tin for 10 minutes, then loosen the sides with the round-bladed knife and turn out on to the wire rack. Remove the lining paper and leave to cool completely.

• Decorate with a little sifted icing sugar and cut into 16 bars to serve. The bars can be stored in an airtight tin for up to 3 days.

tip

★ Swap the sultanas for chocolate dots or diced milk chocolate, if you like.

millionaire's shortbread

makes
18

ingredients

oil, for greasing

250 g (8 oz) plain flour

25 g (1 oz) cornflour

50 g (2 oz) caster sugar

175 g (6 oz) butter, at room temperature

Topping

2 tablespoons golden syrup

75 g (3 oz) butter

75 g (3 oz) light muscovado sugar

3 tablespoons double cream

75 g (3 oz) dark or milk chocolate

75 g (3 oz) white chocolate (optional)

②

equipment

pastry brush

small roasting tin
(see page 12)

kitchen scales and
measuring spoons

large and medium
mixing bowls

round-bladed knife

plate

small saucepan

wooden spoon

dessertspoon

large sharp knife

what to do

1 • Set the oven to 180°C/350°F/Gas Mark 4.

  • Lightly brush the tin with a little oil.

② • Put the flour, cornflour and sugar in the large mixing bowl.

  • Cut the butter into pieces on the plate then add to the bowl. Rub the butter into the flour mixture between your fingertips to make tiny crumbs.

  • Squeeze the crumbs together then tip the mixture into the oiled tin and press flat with your hands.

③ • Bake the shortbread for 20–25 minutes until it is pale golden.

③

- When the shortbread is almost ready, put the golden syrup, butter and sugar in the saucepan and heat until the butter has melted. Boil for 1 minute. Stir in the cream and cook for 30 seconds.

- Pour the hot toffee over the hot shortbread, smooth flat then leave to cool and set.

(4) • To finish, break the dark or milk chocolate into pieces and put in the second bowl. Put this over a saucepan of just boiled water and leave for 4–5 minutes until melted.

- Drizzle spoonfuls of the melted chocolate in wiggly scribble-like lines over the set toffee. Chill for 15 minutes.

- Melt the white chocolate, if using, in the same way as the dark then drizzle over the top. Chill until set. Cut the shortbread into 18 pieces and lift out of the tin.

mini birthday cake squares

equipment

pastry brush

small roasting tin (see page 12)

scissors

greaseproof paper

kitchen scales and measuring spoons

1 large, 1 medium and 2 small mixing bowls

grater

wooden spoon

dessertspoon

round-bladed knife

wire rack

large chopping board

large sharp knife

ingredients

oil, for greasing

250 g (8 oz) soft margarine

250 g (8 oz) caster sugar

250 g (8 oz) self-raising flour

4 eggs

grated rind of 1 lemon or 1 small orange

To finish

100 g (3½ oz) butter, at room temperature

200 g (7 oz) icing sugar

2–4 teaspoons milk

a few drops blue, orange and pink food colouring

24 candles and candle holders

selection of sweets (such as dolly mixtures, mini candy-coated chocolate sweets or mini marshmallows)

sugar strands or hundreds and thousands

what to do

1 • Set the oven to 180°C/350°F/Gas Mark 4.

 • Brush the tin with a little oil, line the base with a rectangle of greaseproof paper and brush this with a little extra oil.

2 • Put all the cake ingredients in the large bowl and beat with the wooden spoon.

 • Spoon into the tin and smooth flat.

3 • Bake the cake for 25–30 minutes until it is well risen and golden brown, and the top springs back when lightly pressed.

- Leave the cake to cool in the tin for about 10 minutes, then loosen the sides with the round-bladed knife and turn out on to the wire rack. Carefully remove the lining paper and leave the cake to cool completely.

4 • To make the icing, beat the butter in the medium bowl with a little of the icing sugar (there is no need to sift it first), then gradually mix in the rest, a few spoonfuls at a time, along with enough milk to make a smooth spreadable icing.

- Divide the icing into 3 and place two of the thirds in the small bowls. Colour one-third of the icing pale blue, one-third pale orange and the rest pale pink.

- Put the cake on the large chopping board and cut into 3 pieces. Spread a different coloured icing over each piece of cake using the round-bladed knife. Cut into 24 small pieces with a large sharp knife.

- Put a candle holder and candle in the centre of each piece then arrange the sweets and sugar strands around it. Store in an airtight tin for up to 2 days.

scottish  shortbread

makes 8

equipment

kitchen scales

large mixing bowl

round-bladed knife

plate

electric mixer (optional)

20 cm (8 inch) fluted-edged, loose-bottomed flan tin

fork

large sharp knife

ingredients

175 g (6 oz) plain flour

125 g (4 oz) butter, at room temperature

50 g (2 oz) caster sugar, plus a little extra for sprinkling

what to do

1 • Set the oven to 160°C/325°F/Gas Mark 3.

• Put the flour in the mixing bowl. Cut the butter into pieces on the plate then add to the flour along with the sugar.

2 • Rub the butter into the flour mixture between your fingertips to make tiny crumbs, or use an electric mixer.

• Squeeze the crumbs together with your hands until they stick together.

3 • Tip the mixture into the tin (there is no need to grease it first) and press flat using your hands.

• Decorate all around the edge of the shortbread by pressing your finger into the edge. Prick the middle with the fork and sprinkle with a little extra sugar.

4 • Bake the shortbread for 20–25 minutes until it is pale golden.

• Take out of the oven and mark into 8 triangular-shaped pieces. Leave the shortbread to cool in the tin.

• Cut the shortbread right through and lift out of the tin. These can be stored in an airtight tin for up to 5 days.

tip

★ If you don't have a flan tin then press the shortbread into a round on a baking sheet.

iced gingerbread and banana slices

(2)

(5)

makes 16

equipment

pastry brush

small roasting tin (see page 12)

scissors

greaseproof paper

kitchen scales and measuring spoons

medium saucepan

wooden spoon

plate

fork

2 small mixing bowls

dessertspoon

round-bladed knife

wire rack

sieve

large sharp knife

ingredients

oil, for greasing

125 g (4 oz) butter

150 g (5 oz) golden syrup

100 g (3½ oz) light muscovado sugar

2 bananas, each about 175 g (6 oz) before peeling

2 eggs

2 tablespoons milk

250 g (8 oz) self-raising flour

2 teaspoons ground ginger

½ teaspoon bicarbonate of soda

To finish

200 g (7 oz) icing sugar

5–6 teaspoons water

few drops pink food colouring (optional)

sugar strands, to decorate

what to do

1 • Set the oven to 180°C/350°F/Gas Mark 4.

• Lightly brush the tin with a little oil, line the base with a rectangle of greaseproof paper and brush this lightly with a little extra oil.

94

2 • Put the butter, syrup and sugar in the saucepan. Heat gently, stirring occasionally with the wooden spoon until melted.

• Meanwhile, peel then mash the bananas on the plate using the fork.

• Put the eggs and milk in one of the small bowls and mix together with the fork.

• Put the flour, ginger and bicarbonate of soda in the other small bowl and mix with the dessertspoon.

3 • Take the pan off the heat, add the flour mixture and bananas and beat until smooth. Add the egg and milk mixture and mix well.

• Pour the cake mixture into the lined tin. Smooth flat with the back of the spoon.

4 • Bake the gingerbread for 20–25 minutes until it is well risen and golden brown, and the top springs back when lightly pressed with a fingertip.

• Leave the gingerbread to cool in the tin for 10 minutes, then loosen the sides with the round-bladed knife and turn out on to the wire rack. Remove the lining paper and leave to cool completely.

5 • To make the icing, sift the icing sugar into a clean bowl. Gradually mix in the water to make a smooth spreadable icing. Colour it pale pink if you'd like.

• Pour the icing over the top of the cake and smooth flat with the round-bladed knife. Decorate with sugar strands.

• Leave for 30 minutes until the icing has set, then cut the gingerbread into 16 bars. The slices can be stored in an airtight tin for up to 3 days.

carrot, honey and sultana squares

makes
15

equipment

pastry brush

small roasting tin
(see page 12)

scissors

greaseproof paper

kitchen scales, measuring
spoons and jug

vegetable peeler

grater

chopping board

large and medium
mixing bowls

fork or balloon whisk

dessertspoon

round-bladed knife

wire rack

lemon squeezer

large sharp knife

ingredients

oil, for greasing

3 carrots, 200 g (7 oz) in
total before peeling

150 ml (¼ pint)
sunflower oil

3 eggs

125 g (4 oz) thick-set or
runny honey

50 g (2 oz) light
muscovado sugar

200 g (7 oz) wholemeal
self-raising flour

2 teaspoons baking
powder

100 g (3½ oz) sultanas

To finish

½ orange

100 g (3½ oz) butter,
at room temperature

200 g (7 oz) icing sugar

large and small candy-
coated chocolate sweets,
to decorate

what to do

(1) • Set the oven to 180°C/350°F/Gas Mark 4.

• Brush the tin with a little oil, line the base
with a rectangle of greaseproof paper and
brush this lightly with a little extra oil.

• Peel then grate the carrots on to the board.

(2) • Put the oil, eggs, honey and sugar in the
large mixing bowl and mix together using
the fork or whisk.

- Add the flour and baking powder and mix well, then stir in the grated carrots and the sultanas with the metal spoon.

- Pour the cake mixture into the lined tin and smooth flat.

3 • Bake the cake for 20–25 minutes until it is well risen and golden brown, and the top springs back when lightly pressed.

- Leave the cake to cool in the tin for 10 minutes, then loosen the sides with the round-bladed knife and turn out on to the wire rack. Remove the lining paper and leave to cool completely.

4 • To make the frosting, finely grate the orange and squeeze the juice.

- Put the butter in the medium mixing bowl, add the orange rind then gradually mix in the icing sugar and some of the orange juice to make a soft spreadable icing.

- Spread the icing over the top of the cake with the round-bladed knife then cut the cake into 15 pieces. Decorate with the sweets. The squares can be stored in an airtight tin for up to 2 days.

cherry streusel cake

cuts into 16 squares

equipment

scissors

nonstick baking paper

20 cm (8 inch) square shallow cake tin

kitchen scales and measuring spoons

large and small mixing bowls

round-bladed knife

plate

electric mixer (optional)

wooden spoon

dessertspoon

sieve

large sharp knife

ingredients

175 g (6 oz) self-raising flour

100 g (3½ oz) butter, at room temperature

75 g (3 oz) caster sugar

50 g (2 oz) ground almonds

1 egg

2 tablespoons milk

½ teaspoon almond essence

425 g (14 oz) can stoned black cherries

25 g (1 oz) flaked almonds

what to do

1 • Set the oven to 180°C/350°F/Gas Mark 4.

• Cut a square of nonstick baking paper a little larger than the tin, then snip into the corners and press the paper into the tin.

2 • Put the flour in the large mixing bowl. Cut the butter into pieces on the plate then add to the flour. Rub the butter into the flour between your fingertips to make tiny crumbs, or use an electric mixer.

• Stir in the sugar and ground almonds.

• Measure out 75 g (3 oz) of the crumb mixture and set aside for the topping in

the second bowl. Add the egg, milk and almond essence to the rest of the mixture and mix together until smooth.

(3) • Spoon the soft cake mixture into the lined tin and smooth flat.

• Tip the cherries into the sieve set over the empty small bowl and drain away the liquid, then spoon the cherries on top of the cake mixture.

• Sprinkle the reserved crumbs and the flaked almonds on top.

4 • Bake the cake for 25–30 minutes until it is well risen and the topping is pale golden.

• Leave the cake to cool in the tin, then loosen the sides and lift out, holding the edges of the paper. Peel away the paper then cut into 16 squares to serve. Store the cake in an airtight tin for up to 2 days.

cakes to impress

strawberry and mascarpone layer cake

equipment

pastry brush

two 20 cm (8 inch) Victoria sandwich tins

scissors

greaseproof paper

kitchen scales and measuring spoons

grater

large, medium and small mixing bowls

wooden spoon

2 dessertspoons

round-bladed knife

wire rack

serving plate

sieve

ingredients

oil, for greasing

175 g (6 oz) soft margarine

175 g (6 oz) caster sugar

175 g (6 oz) self-raising flour

1 teaspoon baking powder

grated rind of 1 lemon

3 eggs

To finish

175 g (6 oz) low-fat mascarpone cheese

2 tablespoons icing sugar, plus a little extra for dusting

400 g (13 oz) strawberries, stalks removed

3 tablespoons strawberry jam

what to do

1 • Set the oven to 180°C/350°F/Gas Mark 4.

• Brush the tins with a little oil, line the bases with circles of greaseproof paper and brush these with a little extra oil.

2 • Put all the cake ingredients in the large bowl and beat with the wooden spoon.

• Divide the mixture equally between the 2 lined tins and smooth flat with the back of a metal spoon.

3 • Bake the cakes for about 20 minutes until they are well risen and golden brown, and the tops spring back when lightly pressed.

• Leave the cakes to cool in the tins for 5 minutes, then loosen the sides with the round-bladed knife and turn out on to the wire rack. Remove the lining paper and leave to cool completely.

4 • To make the filling, put the mascarpone cheese and icing sugar in the medium bowl and beat together until soft.

5 • Put one of the cakes on the serving plate and spread with the cheese mixture.

• Keep back 4 strawberries for the decoration and slice the rest. Mix these with the jam in the small bowl then spoon on top of the cheese mixture. Carefully put the second cake on top.

• Decorate with the reserved strawberries, cut in halves (keeping them in place with a little mascarpone, if necessary) and a little extra sifted icing sugar. The cake is best eaten on the day it is made.

peach melba cake

cuts into
10–12 slices

equipment

pastry brush

20 cm (8 inch) round
springform tin

scissors

greaseproof paper

kitchen scales

small sharp knife

chopping board

grater

large and small bowls

wooden spoon

fork

dessertspoon

teaspoon

skewer

wire rack

serving plate

ingredients

oil, for greasing

3 peaches, about 375 g
(12 oz) in total

200 g (7 oz) butter, at
room temperature

200 g (7 oz) caster sugar

grated rind of 1 lemon

3 eggs

200 g (7 oz) self-raising
flour

125 g (4 oz) raspberries

150 g (5 oz) full-fat
cream cheese

sifted icing sugar, to
decorate

what to do

1 • Set the oven to 160°C/325°F/Gas Mark 3.

• Brush the tin with a little oil, line the base
with greaseproof paper and brush this
with a little extra oil.

• Cut the peaches in half, cut out the stones
and then thinly slice the fruit.

2 • Beat the butter, sugar and rind in the large
bowl with the wooden spoon until fluffy.

• Beat the eggs in the small bowl with the
fork. Slowly add a little egg to the butter
mixture then some flour, beating well after
each addition. Continue until both have
been added. Mix for 1–2 minutes.

• Spoon half the cake mixture into the lined
tin and smooth flat.

(3) • Cover with half the peach slices and half the raspberries then dot all the cream cheese over the top, using the teaspoon.

• Spoon the rest of the cake mixture on top and gently smooth flat.

• Arrange the remaining peach slices and raspberries over the top.

4 • Bake the cake for about 1 hour 10 minutes to 1 hour 25 minutes until it is well risen and a skewer comes out cleanly when pushed into the centre of the cake.

• Leave the cake to cool in the tin for 15 minutes. Loosen the sides with the round-bladed knife, then release the cake and transfer to the wire rack. Remove the lining paper and leave to cool completely.

• Dust the cake with a little sifted icing sugar.

chocolate fudge squares

(4)

(4)

makes
16

equipment

pastry brush

20 cm (8 inch) square
shallow cake tin

scissors

greaseproof paper

kitchen scales and
measuring spoons

large mixing bowl

wooden spoon

dessertspoon

round-bladed knife

wire rack

medium saucepan

large sharp knife

ingredients

oil, for greasing

175 g (6 oz) soft
margarine

175 g (6 oz) caster sugar

150 g (5 oz) self-raising
flour

25 g (1 oz) cocoa powder

½ teaspoon baking powder

3 eggs

To finish

25 g (1 oz) butter

100 g (3½ oz) dark
chocolate

25 g (1 oz) icing sugar

2–3 teaspoons milk

dolly mixtures or candy-
coated chocolate sweets,
to decorate

what to do

1 • Set the oven to 180°C/350°F/Gas Mark 4.

• Brush the tin with a little oil, line the base
with greaseproof paper and brush this
lightly with a little extra oil.

2 • Put all the cake ingredients in the mixing
bowl and beat with the wooden spoon.
Spoon into the tin and smooth flat.

• Bake the cake for 25–30 minutes until it
is well risen and browned, and the top
springs back when lightly pressed.

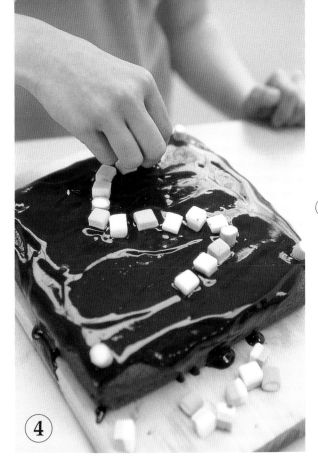

3 • Leave the cake to cool in the tin for 10 minutes, then loosen the sides with the round-bladed knife and turn out on to the wire rack. Remove the lining paper and leave to cool completely.

④ • To make the frosting, heat the butter in the saucepan until just melted. Break the chocolate into squares, add to the pan and heat gently until melted.

• Stir in the icing sugar and heat gently until glossy then stir in enough milk to make a thick spreadable icing. Quickly pour over the top of the cake and spread into an even layer. Decorate with the sweets and mark into 16 squares. Leave the icing to harden for 30 minutes.

• Cut the cake into the marked squares and store in an airtight tin for up to 2 days.

chocolate and orange swirl cake

cuts into
10 slices

equipment

pastry brush

20 cm (8 inch) round
springform tin

scissors

greaseproof paper

kitchen scales and
measuring spoons

small, medium and large
mixing bowls

teaspoon

wooden spoon

tablespoon

grater

round-bladed knife

skewer

wire rack

small saucepan

large plate

ingredients

oil, for greasing

4 teaspoons cocoa
powder

4 teaspoons boiling water

175 g (6 oz) soft
margarine

175 g (6 oz) caster sugar

200 g (7 oz) self-raising
flour

3 eggs

grated rind of ½ orange

To finish

50 g (2 oz) butter

25 g (1 oz) cocoa powder

250 g (8 oz) icing sugar

1–2 tablespoons milk

sugar flowers or
chocolate sweets (such
as segments of chocolate
orange or a sliced
chocolate bar), to
decorate

what to do

1 • Set the oven to 180°C/350°F/Gas Mark 4.

   • Lightly brush the tin with a little oil, line
     the base with a circle of greaseproof paper
     and brush this lightly with a little extra oil.

   • Put the cocoa powder in the small bowl,
     add the boiling water and mix to a paste.

2 • Put the margarine, sugar, flour and eggs in
     the large mixing bowl and beat with the
     wooden spoon until smooth.

- Spoon half the mixture into the medium bowl and stir in the cocoa paste.

- Stir the orange rind into the other half of the cake mixture.

③ • Add alternate spoonfuls of the 2 different cake mixtures to the lined tin then run the round-bladed knife through the colours to marble or swirl them together.

- Bake the cake for 35–40 minutes until it is well risen and golden brown, and a skewer comes out cleanly when pushed into the centre of the cake.

4 • Leave the cake to cool in the tin for 15 minutes. Loosen the sides with the round-bladed knife, then release the cake

and transfer to the wire rack. Remove the lining paper and leave to cool completely.

5 • To make the frosting, put the butter in the small saucepan and heat until melted.

- Stir in the cocoa powder and cook for 1 minute.

- Take off the heat and stir in the icing sugar. Return to the hob and heat for 1 minute until glossy. Stir in enough milk to make a smooth spreadable icing.

- Transfer the cake to a wire rack set over a large plate. Spoon the icing over the top, then smooth evenly with the knife. Decorate with sugar flowers and leave to harden for 30 minutes before slicing. Store in an airtight tin for up to 2 days.

carrot and banana layer cake

④

cuts into
10–12 slices

equipment

pastry brush

20 cm (8 inch) round
deep cake tin

scissors

greaseproof paper

kitchen scales, measuring
spoons and jug

large and small bowls

fork

wooden spoon

grater

2 plates

skewer

round-bladed knife

wire rack

large serrated knife

lemon squeezer

serving plate

ingredients

oil, for greasing

175 g (6 oz) light
muscovado sugar

200 ml (7 fl oz)
sunflower oil

4 eggs

2 carrots, about 200 g
(7 oz) in total, scrubbed

1 small banana, about
150 g (5 oz) before
peeling

75 g (3 oz) sultanas
(optional)

175 g (6 oz) self-raising
flour

175 g (6 oz) wholemeal
self-raising flour

1 teaspoon ground
cinnamon

1 teaspoon baking powder

To finish

400 g (13 oz) full-fat
cream cheese

150 g (5 oz) icing sugar

grated rind of 1 orange

2 tablespoons orange juice

a few banana chips
and a few orange slices,
to decorate

what to do

1 • Set the oven to 180°C/350°F/Gas Mark 4.

• Lightly brush the tin with a little oil, line
the base with a circle of greaseproof paper
and brush this lightly with a little extra oil.

2 • Put the sugar, oil and eggs in the large bowl
and beat with the fork until well mixed.

⑤

- Coarsely grate the carrots on to a plate.

- Peel then mash the banana on the other plate using the fork.

3 • Add the grated carrots and mashed banana to the egg mixture along with the sultanas, if using, and mix together.

- Add the flours, cinnamon and baking powder and mix together.

- Pour the mixture into the lined tin and smooth with the back of the spoon.

④ • Bake the cake for about 1 hour until it is well risen and golden brown, and a skewer comes out cleanly when pushed into the centre of the cake.

- Leave the cake to cool in the tin for 15 minutes, then loosen the sides with the round-bladed knife and turn out on to the wire rack. Remove the lining paper and leave to cool completely.

- Cut the cake horizontally into 3 even-sized layers.

⑤ • To make the frosting, put the cream cheese, icing sugar, orange rind and juice in the second bowl and beat with the wooden spoon until smooth.

- Sandwich the cake layers together with a little of the frosting and spread the rest over the top and sides to completely cover the cake. Transfer to the serving plate.

- Decorate the cake with banana chips and some slices of orange. It is best eaten on the day it is made.

lemon and polenta drizzle cake

equipment

pastry brush

1 kg (2 lb) loaf tin
(see page 12)

scissors

greaseproof paper

kitchen scales and
measuring spoons

large and medium bowls

wooden spoon

fork

grater

skewer

dessertspoon

lemon squeezer

small saucepan

wire rack

small new paintbrush

4 plates

ingredients

oil, for greasing

175 g (6 oz) butter, at
room temperature

150 g (5 oz) caster sugar

3 eggs

175 g (6 oz) self-raising
flour

75 g (3 oz) polenta
grains (cornmeal)

1 teaspoon baking
powder

grated rind of 2 lemons

Lemon syrup

juice of 2 lemons

175 g (6 oz) caster sugar

To finish (optional)

1 dried egg white made
up with warm water
according to packet
directions

a few fresh primroses,
pansies or violas

caster sugar, for
sprinkling

what to do

1 • Set the oven to 180°C/350°F/Gas Mark 4.

• Brush the loaf tin with a little oil, then cut
a piece of greaseproof paper to cover the
base and the 2 longest sides. Place in the
tin and brush lightly with a little extra oil.

2 • Put the butter and sugar in the large
mixing bowl and beat with the wooden
spoon until light and fluffy.

(4)

(5)

- Beat the eggs in the medium bowl with the fork then add alternate spoonfuls of egg and flour to the butter mixture, mixing well until they have all been added. Stir in the polenta, baking powder and lemon rind.

3 - Spoon the cake mixture into the tin and smooth flat with the back of the spoon.

- Bake the cake for 40–50 minutes until it is well risen and golden brown, the top is cracked and a skewer comes out cleanly when pushed into the centre of the cake.

④ - Meanwhile, make the lemon syrup. Put the lemon juice and sugar in the pan and heat gently, stirring until the sugar has dissolved, then boil for 1 minute and set aside.

- Lift the cake out of the tin and put it on the wire rack set over a large plate.

- Make skewer holes in the top of the cake then spoon over the hot lemon syrup so that it runs down into the holes. When all the syrup has been added, leave the cake to cool completely.

⑤ - To finish, make up the dried egg white as the packet instructs, then brush the liquid over the flowers using the paintbrush.

- Holding one flower at a time over a plate, sprinkle a little sugar over the top using the cleaned dessertspoon. Shake off the excess sugar and put the sugared flowers on the other plate to dry.

- Transfer the cake to the serving plate or board, removing the lining paper. Arrange the sugared flowers on top of the cake just before serving – it is best eaten on the day it is made.

blueberry and white chocolate cake

cuts into 10 slices

equipment

pastry brush

1 kg (2 lb) loaf tin (see page 12)

scissors

greaseproof paper

kitchen scales and measuring spoons

plastic bag

rolling pin

large and small bowl

small saucepan

fork

dessertspoon

skewer

round-bladed knife

wire rack

vegetable peeler

serving plate

ingredients

oil, for greasing

175 g (6 oz) white chocolate

250 g (8 oz) plain flour

2½ teaspoons baking powder

125 g (4 oz) caster sugar

50 g (2 oz) butter

2 tablespoons sunflower oil

2 tablespoons milk

3 eggs

1 teaspoon vanilla essence

125 g (4 oz) fresh blueberries, plus a few extra to decorate

what to do

1 • Set the oven to 180°C/350°F/Gas Mark 4.

• Brush the loaf tin with a little oil, then cut a piece of greaseproof paper to go over the base and up the 2 longest sides. Place in the tin and brush with a little extra oil.

• Put 100 g (3½ oz) of the white chocolate in the plastic bag and hit with the rolling pin until broken into small chunks.

2 • Put the flour, baking powder and sugar in the large mixing bowl.

• Melt the butter in the saucepan on the hob. Add the oil, milk, eggs and vanilla essence and mix together with the fork.

• Pour the butter mixture into the dry ingredients and beat with the fork until only just mixed. Stir in the broken chocolate and the blueberries until just mixed.

3 • Spoon the mixture into the tin and smooth flat with the back of the spoon. Bake the cake for 35–45 minutes until it is well risen and golden brown, the top is cracked and a skewer comes out cleanly when pushed into the centre of the cake.

• Leave the cake to cool in the tin for 10 minutes, then loosen the sides with the round-bladed knife and turn out on to the wire rack. Remove the lining paper and leave to cool completely.

4 • To finish the cake, break the rest of the white chocolate into pieces and put in the small mixing bowl. Put this over a saucepan of just boiled water and leave for 4–5 minutes until melted.

• Put the cake on the serving plate then spoon the melted white chocolate over the top. Add a few blueberries to decorate. Leave to harden before cutting into 10 slices to serve. The cake can be stored in an airtight tin for up to 2 days.

celebration chocolate lace cake

(3)

(4)

cuts into
8 slices

equipment

pastry brush

two 20 cm (8 inch)
Victoria sandwich tins

scissors

greaseproof paper

kitchen scales, measuring
spoons and jug

small, medium and large
mixing bowls

dessertspoon

electric or balloon whisk

round-bladed knife

wire rack

saucepan

baking sheet

nonstick baking paper

cake board

ingredients

oil, for greasing

50 g (2 oz) cocoa powder

6 tablespoons boiling
water

150 ml (¼ pint)
sunflower oil

3 eggs

175 g (6 oz) caster sugar

175 g (6 oz) self-raising
flour

1½ teaspoons baking
powder

Chocolate lace

50 g (2 oz) dark or milk
chocolate

50 g (2 oz) white
chocolate

To finish

3 tablespoons chocolate
spread

300 ml (½ pint) double
cream

what to do

1 • Set the oven to 180°C/350°F/Gas Mark 4.

• Lightly brush the tins with a little oil, line
the bases with circles of greaseproof paper
and brush these with a little extra oil.

• Put the cocoa powder in the small bowl,
gradually add the boiling water and mix
to a smooth paste with the dessertspoon.
Set aside to cool.

(5)

2 • Put the oil, eggs and sugar in the large mixing bowl and whisk together. Add the cocoa paste, flour and baking powder and whisk again until smooth.

3 • Divide the mixture equally between the tins and smooth flat with the back of the spoon.

• Bake the cakes for 18–20 minutes until they are well risen and browned, and the tops spring back when lightly pressed.

• Leave the cakes to cool in the tins for 10 minutes, then loosen the sides with the knife and transfer to the wire rack. Remove the paper and leave to cool completely.

4 • Meanwhile, make the chocolate lace. Break the milk chocolate into pieces and put in the medium bowl set over a pan of boiled water. Leave for 5 minutes until melted.

• Line a baking sheet with nonstick baking paper then drizzle the melted chocolate over the paper in wiggly lines. Chill in the fridge for 30 minutes until hard.

• Melt the white chocolate in the same way in the washed bowl then drizzle this over the hard chocolate layer and chill again.

5 • Put one of the cakes on the cake board and spread with the chocolate spread.

• Whip the cream in a mixing bowl using the clean whisk until it has just thickened. Spoon half the cream over the chocolate spread. Cover with the second cake then spread the rest of the cream on top.

• Break the chocolate lace into pieces and stand up at angles over the top of the cake. Cut the cake into slices to serve – it is best eaten on the day it is made.

iced ginger and date sandwich cake

cuts into
10 slices

equipment

pastry brush

20 cm (8 inch) round loose-bottomed tin

scissors

greaseproof paper

kitchen scales, measuring spoons and jug

medium saucepan

wooden spoon

dessertspoon

3 mixing bowls

fork

skewer

wire rack

plate

electric or balloon whisk

large serrated knife

sieve

ingredients

oil, for greasing

100 g (3½ oz) butter

200 g (7 oz) golden syrup

75 g (3 oz) light muscovado sugar

150 g (5 oz) ready-chopped dates

150 ml (¼ pint) milk

100 g (3½ oz) self-raising flour

125 g (4 oz) wholemeal plain or Granary flour

2 teaspoons ground ginger

½ teaspoon bicarbonate of soda

2 eggs

Banana cream filling

1 banana

1 tablespoon lemon juice

150 ml (¼ pint) double cream

To finish

100 g (3½ oz) icing sugar

about 3 teaspoons water

what to do

1 • Set the oven to 160°C/325°F/Gas Mark 3.

• Lightly brush the tin with a little oil, line the base with a circle of greaseproof paper and brush this lightly with a little extra oil.

(6)

(7)

2 • Put the butter, syrup, sugar, dates and milk in the pan and heat gently, stirring with the wooden spoon until the butter has melted and the sugar dissolved.

• Mix the flours, ginger and bicarbonate of soda together in one of the bowls.

• Put the eggs in the other bowl and beat with the fork.

3 • Take the pan off the heat, add the flour mixture and mix until smooth. Add the beaten eggs and beat again until smooth.

4 • Pour the mixture into the tin and cook the cake for about 1 hour until it is well risen and deep brown, and a skewer comes out cleanly when pushed into the centre.

• Leave the cake to cool for 10 minutes, then remove the cake from the tin and transfer to the wire rack. Remove the lining paper and leave to cool completely.

5 • To make the banana cream filling, peel then mash the banana on the plate using the clean fork then mix in the lemon juice.

• Whip the cream in a bowl using the electric or balloon whisk until it has just thickened, but be careful not to overwhip or it will look more like butter.

• Stir in the mashed banana.

(6) • Cut the cake horizontally into 2 layers using the serrated knife, then sandwich them together with the banana cream.

(7) • Sift the icing sugar into one of the cleaned bowls then gradually mix in the water to make a smooth thick icing.

• Drizzle the icing over the top of the cake and leave for 30 minutes to harden. The cake is best eaten on the day it is made.

raspberry swiss roll

cuts into 8 slices

ingredients

4 eggs

125 g (4 oz) caster sugar, plus a little extra for sprinkling

125 g (4 oz) plain flour

To finish

5 tablespoons raspberry jam

150 g (5 oz) fresh or frozen raspberries, just thawed

pink and white sugar flowers, to decorate

equipment

scissors

nonstick baking paper

medium roasting tin (see page 12)

medium saucepan

kitchen scales

large mixing bowl

electric whisk

sieve

large metal spoon

clean tea towel

round-bladed knife

serving plate

what to do

1 • Set the oven to 200°C/400°F/Gas Mark 6.

• Cut a piece of nonstick baking paper a little larger than the tin, then snip into the corners and press the paper into the tin.

• Pour water into the saucepan to come about one-third up the sides then heat up.

2 • Put the eggs and sugar in the bowl then set the bowl over the pan of simmering water. Using the electric whisk beat the eggs and sugar for 5 minutes until very thick and foamy. To check whether it is thick enough, lift the whisk and drizzle a little mixture over the top of the bowl. If the trail stays for a few seconds it is ready.

• Sift the flour over the top, gently fold it into the whisked eggs and sugar with the spoon.

3 • Pour the cake mixture into the tin and ease it into the corners by tipping the tin slightly and very gently using the spoon.

• Bake the cake for 8–10 minutes until it is golden brown and just beginning to shrink away from the paper, and the top spring backs when lightly pressed.

• Meanwhile, wet the tea towel with warm water then wring it out. Put the tea towel on the work surface with one of the short sides facing you.

• Cover the tea towel with a piece of nonstick baking paper then sprinkle lightly with a little sugar.

4 • Tip the cake and the lining paper on to the paper-topped tea towel. Peel away the lining paper and then, working quickly, spread the cake with the jam. Sprinkle with two-thirds of the raspberries.

• Using the paper under the cake and the tea towel to help, roll up the cake from the shortest edge nearest you, gradually peeling away the paper and cloth as you work towards the opposite short edge.

• Wrap the paper tightly around the cake and leave for 1–2 minutes to set the rolled-up shape.

• Transfer the cake to the serving plate and decorate with the remaining raspberries and a few sugar flowers. Cut the cake into thick slices to serve – it is best eaten on the day it is made.

creamy kiwi meringue gâteau

(3)

cuts into
8 slices

equipment

2 baking sheets

scissors

nonstick baking paper

pencil

large and medium
mixing bowls

electric whisk

kitchen scales,
measuring spoons
and jug

teaspoon

cup

dessertspoon

vegetable peeler

small sharp knife

chopping board

serving plate

ingredients

4 egg whites

125 g (4 oz) caster sugar

100 g (3½ oz) light
muscovado sugar

1 teaspoon cornflour

1 teaspoon white wine
vinegar

To finish

4 kiwi fruit

150 g (5 oz) seedless
grapes

300 ml (½ pint) double
cream

what to do

1 • Set the oven to 110°C/225°F/Gas Mark ¼.

• Line the baking sheets with pieces of
nonstick baking paper and draw a 23 cm
(9 inch) circle on one and an 18 cm
(7 inch) circle on the other, using cake
tins as templates to draw around.

2 • Put the egg whites in the large bowl and
whisk using the electric whisk until very
stiff. To test whether they are ready, turn
the bowl upside down – if the eggs look
like they may slide out, whisk for a few
minutes more.

(5)

- Gradually whisk in the sugars, a teaspoonful at a time, and continue whisking for 1–2 minutes more, even when all the sugar has been added, so that the meringue is very thick and glossy.

- Mix the cornflour and vinegar in the cup then whisk into the meringue.

3 • Spoon the meringue on to the lined baking sheets and spread within the marked circles.

- Bake the meringue layers for 1¼ hours or until they can be lifted easily off the paper.

- Leave to cool on the paper. Don't worry if the meringues crack slightly.

4 • To finish the gâteau, peel the brown skin away from the kiwi fruit and discard, then cut the fruit into slices.

- Cut the grapes in half.

- Whip the cream in the second bowl using the cleaned whisk until the cream has thickened and makes soft swirls.

5 • Lift the larger meringue off its lining paper and put on the serving plate. Spread with the cream and arrange the fruit on top.

- Add the other meringue layer and store the gâteau in the fridge until needed – it is best eaten on the day it is made.

baked strawberry and lime cheesecake

1

equipment

scissors

nonstick baking paper

20 cm (8 inch) round
springform tin

small serrated knife

chopping board

grater

lemon squeezer

kitchen scales and
measuring spoons

large and medium
mixing bowls

2 cups or small bowls

electric whisk

dessertspoon

serving plate

ingredients

4 trifle sponges

1 lime

400 g (13 oz) full-fat
cream cheese

125 g (4 oz) caster sugar

2 tablespoons plain flour

4 eggs

To finish

150 g (5 oz) full-fat
crème fraîche

250 g (8 oz) hulled
strawberries

what to do

(1) • Set the oven to 160°C/325°F/Gas Mark 3.

• Line the base and sides of the tin with
nonstick baking paper (see page 12).

• Cut the trifle sponges in half horizontally
and then into triangles. Arrange them
over the base of the tin so that it is
completely covered.

(2) • Finely grate the rind from the lime then
cut in half and squeeze the juice.

2

- Put the cream cheese, sugar and flour in the large mixing bowl.

- Separate the eggs, adding the yolks to the cream cheese mixture and putting the whites in the medium mixing bowl.

- Whisk the egg whites using the electric whisk until they are thick.

- Using the still dirty whisk beat the cream cheese mixture until smooth then beat in the lime rind and juice.

- Gently fold the egg whites into the cream cheese mixture using the metal spoon until evenly mixed.

3
- Pour the mixture into the sponge-lined tin and bake the cheesecake for 50–60 minutes until it is pale golden brown and the centre still wobbles slightly.

- Turn the oven off, open the door slightly and leave the cheesecake in the oven for 15 minutes.

- Take the cheesecake out of the oven and leave to cool completely.

4
- Remove the tin and lining paper from the cheesecake and put it on the plate. Spoon the crème fraîche on top and smooth with the back of the spoon. Decorate with the strawberries and chill until ready to serve.

farmhouse white loaf

(2)

(3)

makes 1 large loaf

equipment

pastry brush

1 kg (2 lb) loaf tin (see page 12)

kitchen scales, measuring spoons and jug

large mixing bowl

wooden spoon

clingfilm

round-bladed knife

wire rack

ingredients

oil, for greasing

500 g (1 lb) strong white flour, plus a little extra for dusting the work surface

½ teaspoon salt

2 teaspoons caster sugar

1 sachet or 2 teaspoons fast-action dried yeast

2 tablespoons sunflower oil

250–300 ml (8–10 fl oz) warm water

what to do

1 • Lightly brush the loaf tin with a little oil.

(2) • Put the flour, salt, sugar and yeast in the mixing bowl.

• Add the oil then gradually mix in just enough of the warm water to mix to a soft but not sticky dough, using the wooden spoon at first then later squeezing together with your hands.

• Sprinkle the work surface with a little flour then knead the dough for 5 minutes until it is smooth and elastic.

(3) • Shape the dough into a sausage shape about the length of the loaf tin with your hands then lift up and press into the oiled tin.

- Cover the top of the dough loosely with lightly oiled clingfilm then leave in a warm place for 30–45 minutes until it has risen just above the top of the tin. Towards the end of the rising time set the oven to 200°C/400°F/Gas Mark 6 to allow it to warm up before using.

4 • Remove the clingfilm and sprinkle the dough with a little flour.

- Bake the bread for 25–30 minutes until it is well risen and golden brown.

- Loosen the sides with the round-bladed knife then turn out and leave to cool on the wire rack. The bread can be stored in a bread bin for up to 2 days.

tip

★ When it is cooked, the base of the loaf should sound hollow when tapped with your fingertips. If the bread feels a little soft on the base after you have turned it out, put it back in the oven without the tin, straight on to the oven shelf, and bake it for 5 more minutes.

soft seeded granary rolls

makes
16

equipment

pastry brush

large baking sheet

kitchen scales,
measuring spoons
and jug

large mixing bowl

wooden spoon

round-bladed knife

clingfilm

ingredients

oil, for greasing

400 g (13 oz) Granary
flour, plus a little extra
for dusting the work
surface

¼ teaspoon salt

1½ teaspoons fast-action
dried yeast

3 teaspoons honey

1 tablespoon olive or
sunflower oil

200–250 ml (7–8 fl oz)
warm water

topping

1 egg yolk

a few sunflower, poppy
and sesame seeds

what to do

1 • Lightly brush the baking sheet with oil.

2 • Put the flour, salt and yeast in the bowl.

• Add the honey and oil then gradually mix
in just enough of the warm water to mix
to a soft but not sticky dough, using the
wooden spoon at first then later squeezing
together with your hands.

③ • Sprinkle the work surface with a little
flour then knead the dough for 5 minutes
until it is smooth and elastic.

• Cut the dough into quarters, then cut each
quarter into 4 more pieces. Shape each
piece into a round ball with your hands.

- Place the balls in rows of 4 on the oiled baking sheet, leaving a little space in between each ball to allow the rolls to rise and spread.

- Cover loosely with lightly oiled clingfilm then leave to rise in a warm place for 30–40 minutes until the rolls are half as big again. Towards the end of the rising time set the oven to 200°C/400°F/Gas Mark 6 to allow it to warm up before using it to cook the bread.

(4)

- Remove the clingfilm and brush the rolls gently with the egg yolk. Sprinkle each row of rolls with a different kind of seed.

- Bake the rolls for 8–10 minutes until they are well risen and browned, and the bases sound hollow when tapped with fingertips.

- Leave the rolls to cool on the baking sheet. Serve them warm or cold with butter – they are best eaten on the day they are made.

herb and sun-dried tomato bread

cuts into
10 slices

equipment

pastry brush

20 cm (8 inch) loose-
bottomed or springform
tin

scissors

kitchen scales,
measuring spoons and
jug

large mixing bowl

wooden spoon

clingfilm

round-bladed knife

wire rack

ingredients

oil, for greasing

small bunch of fresh
chives

3 or 4 sprigs of fresh
rosemary, plus a little
extra for sprinkling

75 g (3 oz) drained sun-
dried tomatoes in oil

200 g (7 oz) strong
white flour, plus a little
extra for dusting the
work surface

200 g (7 oz) Granary
flour, plus a little extra
for sprinkling

¼ teaspoon salt

1 teaspoon caster sugar

1½ teaspoons fast-action
dried yeast

2 tablespoons olive oil or
oil from the sun-dried
tomatoes jar

200–250 ml (7–8 fl oz)
warm water

what to do

(1) • Lightly brush the cake tin with a little oil.

• Snip the chives into pieces with scissors to
fill about 3 tablespoons and the rosemary
to fill about 1 tablespoon then snip the
sun-dried tomatoes into pieces.

2 • Put the flours, salt, sugar and yeast in the
mixing bowl.

• Add the herbs and tomatoes and the oil
then mix in just enough warm water to

make a soft but not sticky dough, using the wooden spoon at first then later squeezing together with your hands.

(3) • Sprinkle the work surface with a little flour then knead the dough for 5 minutes until it is smooth and elastic.

• Shape into a ball then press into the base of the tin. Cover loosely with lightly oiled clingfilm then leave in a warm place for 30–40 minutes until the dough is half as big again or near the top of the tin. Towards the end of the rising time set the oven to 200°C/400°F/Gas Mark 6 to allow it to warm up before using.

4 • Remove the clingfilm and sprinkle the dough with a few extra snipped rosemary leaves and some extra Granary flour.

• Bake the bread for 20–25 minutes until it is deep brown and the base sounds hollow when tapped with fingertips.

• Loosen the edge of the bread with the round-bladed knife. Release from the tin and tip out on to the wire rack. Leave to cool, then slice the bread and serve with cheese or soup.

tip

★ Instead of making a loaf you could cut the dough into 12 pieces and shape them into rolls. Leave the rolls to rise for 30 minutes then sprinkle with flour and cook for 10 minutes.

basil, garlic and cheese twist

③

makes 2 loaves; each cuts into 8 pieces

equipment

pastry brush

large baking sheet

kitchen scales, measuring spoons and jug

large mixing bowl

wooden spoon

rolling pin

round-bladed knife

garlic press

grater

clingfilm

palette knife

wire rack

ingredients

oil, for greasing

400 g (13 oz) strong white flour, plus a little extra for dusting the work surface

¼ teaspoon salt

1 teaspoon caster sugar

1½ teaspoons fast-action dried yeast

2 tablespoons sunflower oil

200–250 ml (7–8 fl oz) warm water

To finish

50 g (2 oz) butter, at room temperature

3 garlic cloves

small bunch of fresh basil

125 g (4 oz) Cheddar cheese

what to do

1 • Lightly brush the baking sheet with oil.

2 • Put the flour, salt, sugar and yeast in the mixing bowl and stir together.

• Add the oil then mix in just enough warm water to make a soft but not sticky dough, using the wooden spoon at first then later squeezing together with your hands.

• Sprinkle the work surface with a little flour then knead the dough for 5 minutes until it is smooth and elastic.

④

(3) • Roll the dough out thinly to make a rectangle about 25 x 45 cm (10 x 18 inches).

• Spread the dough with the butter. Crush the garlic, tear the basil leaves from the stems, keeping a few back for the top of the dough, and sprinkle the garlic and basil over the butter.

• Grate the cheese then sprinkle over the dough, keeping a little back for the top of the dough.

(4) • Roll up the dough from one of the longest edges over to the other.

• Twist the dough several times then cut in half to make 2 long loaves.

5 • Put the loaves on the oiled baking sheet, leaving a little space in between them. Sprinkle with the reserved basil leaves and cheese.

• Cover loosely with lightly oiled clingfilm then leave in a warm place for 30 minutes to rise. Towards the end of the rising time set the oven to 200°C/400°F/Gas Mark 6 to allow it to warm up before using.

• Remove the clingfilm and bake the loaves for 15 minutes until golden brown and the bases sound hollow when tapped with fingertips.

• Loosen the bread with the palette knife then transfer to the wire rack. Serve the bread warm or cold, thickly sliced, with barbecued meats and salad or with bowls of soup. It is best eaten on the day it is made.

sausage pizza squares

equipment

pastry brush

2 large baking sheets

kitchen scales, measuring spoons and jug

large mixing bowl

wooden spoon

rolling pin

small sharp knife

round-bladed knife

chopping board

grater

ingredients

oil, for greasing

400 g (13 oz) strong white flour, plus a little extra for dusting the work surface

¼ teaspoon salt

1 teaspoon caster sugar

1½ teaspoons fast-action dried yeast

2 tablespoons olive oil

200–250 ml (7–8 fl oz) warm water

Pizza topping

4 tablespoons tomato sauce (ketchup)

3 fresh tomatoes

small bunch of fresh basil

4 cooked sausages

4 chilled frankfurters

75 g (3 oz) Cheddar cheese

what to do

1 • Lightly brush the baking sheets with a little oil.

2 • Put the flour, salt, sugar and yeast in the large mixing bowl.

  • Add the oil then gradually mix in just enough of the warm water to mix to a soft but not sticky dough, using the wooden spoon at first then later squeezing together with your hands.

④

④

3 • Sprinkle the work surface with a little flour then knead the dough for 5 minutes until it is smooth and elastic.

• Roll the dough out very thinly to a roughly shaped rectangle, about 37.5 x 25 cm (15 x 10 inches), then cut into 6 smaller equal-sized squares.

• Transfer the squares to the baking sheets, leaving a little space in between to allow the dough to rise and spread.

④ • Spread the top of the pizzas with the tomato sauce, leaving a border of dough still showing.

• Cut the tomatoes into small pieces on the chopping board, arrange on top of the tomato sauce then tear the basil into pieces and sprinkle on the top.

• Thinly slice the cooked sausages and thickly slice the frankfurters. Arrange on top of the tomatoes then grate the cheese and sprinkle on top.

• Leave the pizzas in a warm place to rise (uncovered) for 30 minutes. Towards the end of the rising time set the oven to 220°C/425°F/Gas Mark 7 to allow it to warm up before using.

5 • Bake the pizzas for 10–12 minutes until the cheese is bubbling. Serve the pizzas warm with cucumber and carrot sticks – they are best eaten on the day they are made.

sultana  soda bread

makes 1
round loaf;
cuts into 8
thick slices

equipment

pastry brush

baking sheet

kitchen scales,
measuring spoons
and jug

large mixing bowl

wooden spoon

small saucepan or
microwave-proof bowl

rolling pin

sharp knife

clean tea towel or wire
rack

ingredients

oil, for greasing

150 g (5 oz) Granary or
wholemeal plain flour

175 g (6 oz) plain flour,
plus a little extra for
dusting the work surface

pinch of salt

2 teaspoons cream of
tartar

1 teaspoon bicarbonate
of soda

50 g (2 oz) light
muscovado sugar

125 g (4 oz) sultanas

25 g (1 oz) butter

175–200 ml (6–7 fl oz)
warm milk

what to do

1 • Set the oven to 200°C/400°F/Gas Mark 6.

   • Lightly brush the baking sheet with oil.

2 • Put the flours, salt, cream of tartar,
bicarbonate of soda, sugar and sultanas
in the mixing bowl and mix together.

③ • Melt the butter in the saucepan on the
hob, or in the bowl in the microwave on
full power for 30 seconds.

   • Add the melted butter to the flour mixture
then gradually mix in just enough of the
warm milk to mix to a soft and slightly
sticky dough.

③

④

4 • Sprinkle the work surface with a little flour then knead the dough for 1 minute until it is just smooth.

• Roll out the dough to make a thick 15 cm (6 inch) circle.

• Put on the oiled baking sheet and score a cross right over the top.

• Sprinkle with a little plain flour then bake the bread for about 25 minutes until it is well risen and browned, and the base sounds hollow when tapped.

5 • Wrap in the clean tea towel and leave to cool for a soft crust or, for a crisp crust, leave the loaf to cool unwrapped on the wire rack. Serve the bread warm or cold, thickly sliced and spread with butter. It is best eaten on the day it is made although any leftovers can be toasted on the following day.

tip

★ Mixed dried fruit, chopped dried apricots, peaches or dates could also be added in place of the sultanas.

fruited tea ring

(5)

ingredients

oil, for greasing

400 g (13 oz) strong white flour, plus a little extra for dusting the work surface

¼ teaspoon salt

1 tablespoon light muscovado sugar

1½ teaspoons fast-action dried yeast

2 tablespoons sunflower oil

200–250 ml (7–8 fl oz) warm water

To finish

50 g (2 oz) butter, at room temperature

4 tablespoons light muscovado sugar

grated rind and juice of ½ orange

50 g (2 oz) glacé cherries, plus a few extra for decorating

75 g (3 oz) ready-to-eat dried apricots, plus a few extra for decorating

75 g (3 oz) mixed dried fruit or sultanas

milk, for glazing

125 g (4 oz) icing sugar

a few strips of angelica, to decorate

serves
8

equipment

pastry brush

large baking sheet

kitchen scales, measuring spoons and jug

large and small bowls

wooden spoon

rolling pin

round-bladed knife

grater

small sharp knife

scissors

clingfilm

wire rack

sieve

lemon squeezer

dessertspoon

serving plate

what to do

1 • Lightly brush the baking sheet with oil.

2 • Put the flour, salt, sugar and yeast in the large mixing bowl.

• Add the oil then mix in just enough of the warm water to make a soft but not sticky dough, using the wooden spoon at first then squeezing together with your hands.

(5)

3 • Sprinkle the work surface with a little flour then knead the dough for 5 minutes until it is smooth and elastic.

• Roll out the dough thinly to make a large rectangle, 25 x 45 cm (10 x 18 inches).

4 • Spread the dough with the butter then sprinkle with the sugar and orange rind.

• Cut the cherries into small pieces. Snip the apricots into small pieces with scissors. Sprinkle the cherries, apricots and mixed dried fruit over the dough.

5 • Starting from one of the longest edges, roll up the dough. Stick the edges together with a little milk brushed on.

• Lift the dough on to the baking sheet and shape into a large ring, squeezing the ends together and sticking in place with milk.

• Using the scissors, make 8 small cuts in the dough at intervals around the outside edge.

• Cover loosely with oiled clingfilm then leave to rise in a warm place for 30–40 minutes until the dough is half as big again. Near the end of the rising time set the oven to 200°C/400°F/Gas Mark 6.

6 • Remove the clingfilm, brush the dough with a little milk and bake the bread ring for 15 minutes until it is golden brown and the base sounds hollow when tapped. Carefully transfer to the wire rack to cool.

• To make the icing, sift the icing sugar into the small bowl then gradually mix in the orange juice to make a smooth icing.

• Put the ring on the serving plate, spoon the icing over the top then decorate with the extra pieces of cherry and dried apricot to look like flowers and use the angelica for the flower 'stems'. Leave for 30 minutes then cut the ring into thick slices – it is best eaten on the day it is made.

sticky glazed orange starbursts

makes 20

equipment

kitchen scales, measuring spoons and jug

pestle and mortar or mug and rolling pin

small saucepan

pastry brush

2 large baking sheets

clingfilm

large mixing bowl

grater

wooden spoon

round-bladed knife

scissors

lemon squeezer

wire rack

ingredients

2 teaspoons coriander seeds

25 g (1 oz) butter

500 g (1 lb) strong white flour, plus a little extra for dusting the work surface

1 teaspoon caster sugar

1 teaspoon salt

grated rind of 1 orange

1½ teaspoons fast-action dried yeast

250–300 ml (8–10 fl oz) warm water

To finish

juice of ½ orange

2 tablespoons thick or runny honey

crushed sugar lumps and grated orange rind, to decorate (optional)

what to do

(1) • Crush the coriander seeds using a pestle and mortar or by putting the seeds in the mug and grinding them with the end of the rolling pin.

• Melt the butter in the pan on the hob. Use a little butter to brush over the baking sheets and 2 large sheets of clingfilm.

2 • Put half the coriander seeds in the bowl. Add the flour, sugar, salt, orange rind and yeast and mix together.

- Pour the remaining butter into the flour mixture. Gradually mix in enough of the warm water to mix to a soft but not sticky dough, using the wooden spoon at first and later squeezing together in your hands.

(3) • Sprinkle the work surface with a little flour then knead the dough for 5 minutes until it is smooth and elastic.

- Cut into 20 pieces then shape each piece into a ball.

- Using scissors, make 5 cuts around the edge of each ball, but not right into the centre. Transfer the balls to the baking sheets, leaving a little space in between to allow the rolls to rise and spread.

4 • Sprinkle the rolls with the rest of the coriander seeds. Cover loosely with the buttered clingfilm and leave to rise in a warm place for 30–40 minutes until the rolls are half as big again. Near the end of the rising time set the oven to 200°C/400°F/Gas Mark 6 to allow it to warm up.

5 • Remove the clingfilm and bake the rolls for 10 minutes until golden brown and the bases sound hollow when tapped.

- Meanwhile, make an orange glaze by warming the orange juice and honey together in the cleaned pan until melted.

- Transfer the hot rolls to the wire rack and brush with the honey mixture. Sprinkle them with the crushed sugar lumps and extra grated orange rind, if you like – they are best eaten on the day they are made.

deep-pan fruit salad pizza

(3)

serves 6–8

equipment

pastry brush

28 cm (11 inch) loose-bottomed flan tin

kitchen scales, measuring spoons and jug

large and medium mixing bowls

small saucepan or microwave-proof bowl

wooden spoon

dessertspoon

vegetable peeler

small sharp knife

chopping board

lemon squeezer

kitchen foil

sieve

ingredients

oil, for greasing

300 g (10 oz) strong white flour, plus a little extra for dusting the work surface

pinch of salt

2 tablespoons caster sugar

1½ teaspoons fast-action dried yeast

25 g (1 oz) butter

1 egg

125–150 ml (4–5 fl oz) warm water

Topping

4 tablespoons strawberry jam

2 dessert apples

2 tablespoons lemon juice

2 ripe plums

3 small peaches

25 g (1 oz) butter

2 tablespoons caster sugar

sifted icing sugar, for dusting

what to do

1 • Lightly brush the flan tin with a little oil.

2 • Put the flour, salt, sugar and yeast in the large bowl.

• Melt the butter in the saucepan on the hob, or in the medium bowl in the microwave on full power for 30 seconds.

(3)

- Add the butter and the egg to the flour mixture then slowly mix in just enough warm water to make a soft but not sticky dough. Use the wooden spoon at first then squeeze the dough with your hands.

(3) • Sprinkle the work surface with a little flour then knead the dough for 5 minutes until it is smooth and elastic.

- Put the dough in the tin and press over the base with your hands. Spoon on the jam.

(4) • Quarter, core and peel the apples, then cut each piece in half again. Put in the cleaned medium bowl and toss in the lemon juice.

- Cut the plums and peaches into halves. Cut away the stones. Thickly slice the fruit and arrange the 3 different fruits in rings on top of the pizza dough.

- Leave in a warm place for the dough to rise (uncovered) for 30–40 minutes. Towards the end of the rising time set the oven to 200°C/400°F/Gas Mark 6 to allow it to warm up before using.

5 • Melt the butter as before, brush over the fruit and sprinkle with the caster sugar.

- Bake the pizza for 15 minutes then reduce the oven temperature to 180°C/350°F/Gas Mark 4 and cook for 20–30 minutes more until the base is cooked. Check the pizza and cover with foil if it is browning too quickly.

6 • When cooked, dust the pizza with icing sugar and remove it from the hot tin. Cut it into wedges and serve warm or cold – it is best eaten on the day it is made.

index

acknowledgements

Photography © Octopus Publishing Group Ltd/Vanessa Davies

Food Styling Sara Lewis

Executive Editor Nicky Hill

Editor Jessica Cowie

Executive Art Editor Rozelle Bentheim

Designer One 2 Six Creative

Senior Production Controller Manjit Sihra